NORTHAMPTON TOWN
A Season in the Sun
1964-65

DESERT ISLAND FOOTBALL HISTORIES

CLUB HISTORIES	ISBN
Aberdeen: A Centenary History 1903-2003	1-874287-57-0
Aberdeen: Champions of Scotland 1954-55	1-874287-65-1
Aberdeen: The European Era – A Complete Record	1-874287-11-2
Bristol City: The Modern Era – A Complete Record	1-874287-28-7
Bristol City: The Early Years 1894-1915	1-874287-74-0
Cambridge United: The League Era – A Complete Record	1-905328-06-0
Cambridge United: 101 Golden Greats	1-874287-58-9
The Story of the Celtic 1888-1938	1-874287-15-5
Chelsea: Champions of England 1954-55	1-874287-94-5
Colchester United: Graham to Whitton – A Complete Record	1-874287-27-9
Coventry City: The Elite Era – A Complete Record	1-874287-83-X
Coventry City: An Illustrated History	1-874287-59-7
Dundee: Champions of Scotland 1961-62	1-874287-86-4
Dundee United: Champions of Scotland 1982-83	1-874287-99-6
History of the Everton Football Club 1878-1928	1-874287-14-7
Halifax Town: From Ball to Lillis – A Complete Record	1-874287-26-0
Hereford United: The League Era – A Complete Record	1-874287-18-X
Hereford United: The Wilderness Years 1997-2004	1-874287-83-X
Huddersfield Town: Champions of England 1923-1926	1-874287-88-0
Ipswich Town: The Modern Era – A Complete Record	1-874287-43-0
Ipswich Town: Champions of England 1961-62	1-874287-63-5
Kilmarnock: Champions of Scotland 1964-65	1-874287-87-2
Leyton Orient: A Season in the Sun 1962-63	1-905328-05-2
Luton Town at Kenilworth Road: A Century of Memories	1-905328-10-9
Luton Town: The Modern Era – A Complete Record	1-874287-90-2
Luton Town: An Illustrated History	1-874287-79-1
Manchester United's Golden Age 1903-1914: Dick Duckworth	1-874287-92-9
The Matt Busby Chronicles: Manchester United 1946-69	1-874287-96-1
Motherwell: Champions of Scotland 1931-32	1-874287-73-2
Northampton Town: A Season in the Sun 1965-66	1-905328-01-X
Norwich City: The Modern Era – A Complete Record	1-874287-67-8
Peterborough United: The Modern Era – A Complete Record	1-874287-33-3
Peterborough United: Who's Who?	1-874287-48-1
Plymouth Argyle: The Modern Era – A Complete Record	1-874287-54-6
Plymouth Argyle: 101 Golden Greats	1-874287-64-3
Plymouth Argyle: Snakes & Ladders – Promotions and Relegations	1-874287-82-1
Portsmouth: The Modern Era	1-905328-08-7
Portsmouth: From Tindall to Ball – A Complete Record	1-874287-25-2
Portsmouth: Champions of England – 1948-49 & 1949-50	1-874287-50-3
The Story of the Rangers 1873-1923	1-874287-95-3
The Romance of the Wednesday 1867-1926	1-874287-17-1
Stoke City: The Modern Era – A Complete Record	1-874287-76-7
Stoke City: 101 Golden Greats	1-874287-55-4
Potters at War: Stoke City 1939-47	1-874287-78-3
Swansea City: Seasons in the Sun	1-905328-02-8
Third Lanark: Champions of Scotland 1903-04	1-905328-03-6
Tottenham Hotspur: Champions of England 1950-51, 1960-61	1-874287-93-7
West Ham: From Greenwood to Redknapp	1-874287-19-8
West Ham: The Elite Era – A Complete Record	1-905328-07-9
Wimbledon: From Southern League to Premiership	1-874287-09-0
Wimbledon: From Wembley to Selhurst	1-874287-20-1
Wimbledon: The Premiership Years	1-874287-40-6
Wrexham: The European Era – A Complete Record	1-874287-52-X

WORLD CUP HISTORIES	
England's Quest for the World Cup – A Complete Record	1-874287-61-9
Scotland: The Quest for the World Cup – A Complete Record	1-897850-50-6
Ireland: The Quest for the World Cup – A Complete Record	1-897850-80-8

MISCELLANEOUS	
Red Dragons in Europe – A Complete Record	1-874287-01-5
The Book of Football: A History to 1905-06	1-905328-00-1
Football's War & Peace: The Tumultuous Season of 1946-47	1-874287-70-8

NORTHAMPTON TOWN

A Season in the Sun
1964-65

Series Editor: Clive Leatherdale

Mark Beesley

DESERT ISLAND BOOKS

First published in 2005
by
DESERT ISLAND BOOKS LIMITED
7 Clarence Road, Southend on Sea, Essex SS1 1AN
United Kingdom
www.desertislandbooks.com

© 2005 Mark Beesley

The right of Mark Beesley to be identified as author of this work has been
asserted under The Copyright Designs and Patents Act 1988

British Library Cataloguing-in-Publication Data
A catalogue record for this book is available from the British Library

ISBN 1-905328-01-X

Printed in Great Britain
by
Biddles Ltd

The photographs in this book were kindly provided by the *Northampton Chronicle &
Echo*, Pete Norton, Dave Walden, Mark Gray and David Instone

CONTENTS

FOREWORD

I joined the Cobblers in the summer of 1961 from Exeter City and the following six years at the County Ground were the happiest of my time in football, as well as the most successful in the club's history. The great Dave Bowen and his chief scout Bob Calder came down to Exeter and offered me £20 a week wages, and the club found me a house right behind the rugby ground for thirty shillings a week (£1.50).

Northampton had just been promoted from the old Fourth Division, while Exeter had finished in the bottom four, so it seemed like a good move, even though the Midlands was unknown territory for me and my wife and young daughter. And so it proved. It was a homely and friendly club and Dave was a lovely man with excellent knowledge and judgment, who I learned an awful lot from.

I did know from Exeter's visits that the County Ground could be a cold old place, which it certainly was one night, when the mighty Sunderland, chasing promotion, came down for a game that summed up the spirit of 'little' Northampton. The pitch was covered in ice and the cricket side, always the coldest part, was like glass. Dave Bowen had done well to persuade the referee we should play and when I went to toss up for ends with Sunderland's captain, my old Republic of Ireland team-mate Charlie Hurley, he laughed at the fact I was in plimsolls. 'You're not wearing those Theo!' he said. Sunderland's trainer had forgotten to pack rubber boots, so their players were wearing short studs on the ice. Result: 'Little' Northampton 5 Sunderland 1.

It was a great thrill to be able to upset so many of the big boys in those five glorious years. I hope this book will bring back many memories of a time when we put the town and the football club on the map, and will inspire those too young to remember it.

THEO FOLEY

AUTHOR'S NOTE

People love to share memories. Most too, love a good story. At a time when the pieces of this book were loosely whirring around my head, like so many colourful specks in a kaleidoscope, I attended the funeral of a friend who had been a horse-racing fanatic for more than sixty years. As a group of us sheltered from the rain outside the crematorium, a fellow mourner, a few years younger than the much-loved departed, broke the weighty silence which the occasion and the weather had shrouded over us. 'The last time I saw Sammy he came up to me and asked whether I remembered the bunch finish to the 1937 Lincoln. For heaven's sake, how old did he think I was?'

Of course all Sammy had wanted to do was share some of his most golden memories, and as we get older, that becomes more treasured, yet increasingly difficult to achieve. For Northampton Town supporters, the story of the 1960s will always cast a wider net. The rise and fall from Division Four to Division One and back again, neatly condensed within those years, is a remarkable tale. Unhappily, my own memories of the Cobblers' one season in Division One are non-existent as I was growing up in Northampton at the time, too young to squeeze onto the terraces, which began filling from mid-day during that halcyon era.

However, I notice that the Cobblers recorded victories two days either side of the day I was born in 1961, beating Wrexham 3-0 and Gillingham 1-0. A glance at the archives of club historian Frank Grande also informs me that I celebrated my fourth birthday on the day of the 2-2 draw with Derby at the County Ground. Northampton Town were then one week away from booking a place in Division One for the first and only time, a feat they clinched by thumping Bury 4-1 at Gigg Lane on 17 April 1965.

I have the consolation of knowing that my relative Michael Beesley was at the time covering the club's fortunes for the town's evening paper, the *Chronicle & Echo*. When I first saw the Cobblers for real it was 1968, and they were taking a short pause for breath on the down escalator. By the time Bobby Moore had his hands on the Jules Rimet Trophy, on 30 July 1966, Northampton Town were already back in Division Two and by 1969 had completed the descent, returning to Division Four.

Two stops going up, only one on the way down. On a Snakes & Ladders board, the upheaval is a little more unpredictable. At least the Cobblers' journey had a certain symmetry, a slow and deliberate cruise to the top, followed by a short but breathtaking plummet. Imagine what it must have been like for a club weaned on the bread and dripping world of Hartlepool, Aldershot and Exeter to suddenly sample the caviar and champagne lifestyle of Everton, Arsenal and Manchester United.

Close your eyes and cling on to all of this for just a brief second, then enter the world of freefall. Downwards, (it seems) ever down, returning once more to football's basement.

In compiling my account of this fascinating journey, I am indebted to a number of people who have backed me every inch of the way. At the top of the list comes Frank Grande for his numerous anecdotes, statistics and cups of tea, but my other chief supporters include my wife Caroline, club photographer Pete Norton, Dave Walden for his amazing collection of memorabilia, the *Northampton Chronicle & Echo*, the *Kettering Evening Telegraph* and all at Northampton Town Football Club. Finally I would like to thank Clive Leatherdale of Desert Island Books for proposing this book to me.

MARK BEESLEY

Introduction

I've always maintained that hindsight is a wonderful thing, while not quite in the same league as chicken jalfrezi. Perhaps luckily, hindsight isn't digestible, otherwise life's order might be somewhat different, or at the very least create chronic heartburn. Instead, hindsight is an ability to look back on events, possibly armed with recently acquired information, and tell yourself 'I should have seen that one coming'.

If we were all blessed with hindsight, very few people would ever step into the path of a car and goalkeepers would never be beaten on their near post. So it's surprising, given what he achieved during the early part of the 1960s – which qualified him as some sort of miracle worker – that David Lloyd Bowen never saw my approach on the horizon. He should have known that, one day, I would attempt to write the story of his finest hours and achievement.

The clues were scattered around. In later years, when I knew him best, he talked about it often. I was in earshot a good deal, if too lacking in bravado and worldly experience then, to seize the initiative. Yet this was the mission for me, and it has persistently nagged away since his death on 25 September 1995, at the age of 67.

After all, hadn't I grown up in Thornby Drive in Northampton, just five doors away from the Bowens at No 15 in the early 1960s, at the start of the meteoric rise? As I tried to juggle my first football on Kingsthorpe Rec, I was within hailing distance of the man who marked Pele during the 1958 World Cup quarter-final between Wales and Brazil.

Disappointingly, it seems we rather lost touch for a while. Well actually, around twenty years. The Bowens abandoned Kingsthorpe in 1966 for Woodland Avenue three miles away. There, close to the peaceful undulations of Abington Park and its boating lake – but equally bordering the county's footballing and cricketing mecca which was the County Ground – they lived for 22 years.

That had the advantage of keeping one arm of the Beesley family at bay, while allowing Bowen to devote more time to Northampton Town Football Club, as the challenges and demands brought on by promotions away from football's basement grew ever more daunting.

Being a stone's throw from his working base ironically gave him even less time at home. If he wasn't away scouting for club or country, for Northampton or Wales, he was always tempted to spend more time in the office. And if Bowen missed the pesterings of a small schoolboy, he rarely talked about it. He had the consolation of daily contact with my father's cousin, Michael, who for four years was the Cobblers' correspondent for the town's evening newspaper, the *Chronicle & Echo*.

From 1968, through the 1970s and early 1980s, Bowen remained blissfully unaware that I was one of the suffering few on the terraces as the Cobblers plunged back to Division Four, briefly flirting with stardom again with Bill Dodgin's promotion side of 1975-76, a flickering light which merely prompted immediate demise.

These were largely abject years. I have a vague recollection of spending my 21st birthday watching a forgettable 0-0 draw with Aldershot. By now Bowen had adopted a 'libero' role as general manager and secretary, with which he persevered until he became club President in 1990. One of his regular chores in the early 1980s was to bank the club's match-day takings at the George Row offices of Lloyds Bank, where I then worked.

Imagine his surprise when, one frosty February morning in 1982, he arrived to witness my grinning, inane face looking down on him as he visited. I was still celebrating a 1-0 win over Bury the night before. The crowd had been only 2,109 on a chilly night and the contest had been won with an own-goal.

Still, the die had been cast. My role of 'stalker' intensified when I underwent a career change two years later. As a cub reporter for the weekly *Northants Post*, my tasks involved probing trips to the County Ground to unearth the latest news on injuries and new signings. If Bowen was surprised to see the bank cashier swapping his finger sponge for a notepad and pen he didn't show it.

Let's face it, a man who could pull off such strokes as the 'Sunderland baseball boot ploy' (see The Only Way is Up) and who was capable of having the pitch flooded by the local fire brigade before a Saturday fixture, because we had a better record under floodlights, was not going to be put off by the attentions of an inexperienced young hack. If the only scoops I unearthed in my first year concerned cricket and ice-cream, I didn't feel disgraced. At least I was learning the ground rules.

It was Bowen's friend and teammate Joe Mercer who once described Northampton Town's season of Division One as the 'miracle' of that decade, and the relationship between those two men is an important pointer when trying to fathom exactly how it came about. I hesitate before offering the words 'famously described', as very little about the Cobblers before that meteoric rise, or since, has touched the broader public conscience.

Of course, there have been brief moments of euphoria along the way. FA Cup adventures bringing fifth-round appearances in 1912, 1934, 1950 and 1970 have been scattered among championships in 1963 (Division

Three) and 1987 (Division Four). And many supporters still rejoice in the 3-1 FA Cup giant-killing over an Arsenal side including Bowen in 1958, before a memorable roll in the snow at Liverpool in the fourth round, where pride remained intact despite a 1-3 exit. Yet there have been too many puzzling gaps, rendering those flash points all too infrequent amid years of mediocrity. Lack of investment is usually cited as one reason. Cruel fate is another.

Let's face it, if you were planning to immortalise your football club in the annals of history, would you honestly choose 1965-66 as a defining season, casting aside England's 4-2 World Cup final victory over West Germany in July, in memo form or under 'Any Other Business'?

That's rather like submitting a typed-up press release previewing the village garden fete during the week the church is struck by lightning, or the vicar runs off with the warden. Not by choice, it must be said, but it seems that if the answer is 'Northampton Town', the question must be: 'Which English league football club chose to bury its finest hour in the shadow of the country's most celebrated success?'

Modern supporters might find it hard to grasp that the Cobblers encountered each of England's eleven World Cup heroes at least once during that season. Hurst may have become the nation's hero with a hat-trick to beat the Germans, but he only netted from a penalty-kick in two matches against Bowen's braves in 1965-66, and the Cobblers emerged from those West Ham scrapes with three points out of four.

Not only that, but the team carved out unlikely results against Arsenal, Manchester United, Liverpool and Leeds, and completed a league 'double' over Aston Villa. They did it, also, from one of the least inspiring homes in the country. There's no doubt these *parvenus* caused ripples of resentment among the elite, and that their quick return to Division Two was warmly welcomed in the corridors of power.

The rise of the Cobblers, and their equally dramatic fall, was indeed a 'soccer miracle'. Those with claret and white blood coursing through their veins have Mercer to thank for putting the whole affair into its proper perspective. The man who briefly managed England in 1974 was well qualified to make such a statement, though it wasn't he who took Northampton to Division One in 1965. It was Bowen who did that.

Bowen's association with the boot and shoe town had begun almost twenty years earlier, when he moved with his parents, Bryn and Martha, from South Wales at the end of the Second World War. Health considerations persuaded Bryn that a life in the coal mines had no future, while running the Roadmender Youth Club near Northampton town centre probably did.

It was there that Bowen met his future wife, Audrey. While the boys congregated in one part of the club practising woodwork, the girls had cookery lessons before everyone joined in the middle at 9pm for an hour of convivial dancing.

Also at the club at that time was young Des O'Connor, who became a ball boy at the County Ground, earning sixpence a match. He even had a trial for the reserves as a winger, while his enthusiasm for the club brought him to the ground on non-match days: (as he relates in his auto-biography *Bananas Can't Fly*) 'cleaning boots, tidying up, anything just to be there. I got the same kind of buzz from the football ground that I later felt back stage at the theatre.' O'Connor played for the Cobblers' Colts in the local United Counties League, admitting: 'I was never talented or strong enough to make it to the top flight.' He revealed Bowen's own succinct assessment: 'It's great to be fast Des, but it does help if you take the ball with you!'

As a teenager, Bowen played for the Roadmender Club in the local Town League, but his football career was fashioned in earnest at the County Ground, albeit in unspectacular style. He made just twelve first-team appearances under the management of Tom Smith, split equally between 1947-48 and 1948-49. His debut was in the 2-3 defeat at Notts County on 3 April 1948. The 30,903 crowd was the largest to watch the Cobblers since their fifth round FA Cup defeat at Preston in 1934.

National Service meant Bowen's spell in the RAF between 1946-48 brought him into contact with Pat Whittaker, the son of Arsenal manager Tom, who spent nine years in charge at Highbury between 1947-56. On the recommendation of his buddy Pat, Bowen joined the Highbury groundstaff in 1950 and was largely lost to the Northampton public for another nine years.

Bowen's first four years at Arsenal were as understudy to Scottish international Alex Forbes and Mercer, a bandy legged wing-half dubbed 'The Smiling Tiger' and already a footballing legend. In 1950-51 Bowen replaced Forbes for the final seven games, and when Arsenal were Champions in 1952-53, Bowen played just twice.

Although Bowen made sporadic appearances in the first team, it was a broken leg suffered by Mercer in a 3-0 win over Liverpool in April 1954 which cemented his place. Bowen played in that match, but the following Friday he was wearing Mercer's No 6 shirt in a 3-0 win over Portsmouth. Bowen forged a lasting friendship with Mercer which lasted until Joe's death in 1990. I have an ingrained memory of seeing a frail Mercer after a goalless draw between Tranmere and Northampton in May of that year, which relegated the boot and shoe town to Division Four.

So while Mercer's 'miracle' quote might have been over-stated, he was acutely aware of the financial restraints with which Bowen was inevitably saddled at the County Ground. Mercer appreciated the enormity of the leap by a club who had been founder members of Division Three in 1920 and stayed put ever since.

How ironic that at the moment the Cobblers dropped from Division One in 1966, Mercer – whose previous management jobs had been with Sheffield United and Aston Villa – was passing in the opposite direction after his first season at Manchester City.

How ironic also, that one of Mercer's first signings had been Mike Summerbee for £30,000 from Swindon in August 1965. Bowen had been anxious to sign the winger as Northampton prepared for Division One. Lack of funds meant the move never happened. Colin Bell was another player whose name remained on Bowen's short-list until Bell switched from Bury to City in March 1966. So, many thanks to Mercer!

That 'miracle' catchphrase means that mature Northampton fans can almost dismiss Yuri Gagarin becoming the first man in space in 1961 as irrelevant. After all, the Russian cosmonaut admitted to being less affected by orbiting the earth than by being presented to the teams before the Cobblers' 2-2 draw with Koskis during their Czech tour in May 1965.

As for Neil Armstrong's moon landing in 1969, there's a popularly held belief on Walter Tull Way that Mission Control was not observing a game of golf on the moon but conveying the thoughts of the awestruck sporting world when remarking: 'I never thought they'd get down in three [66-69].'

And what of The Beatles? Was it simply coincidence that *Ticket To Ride* entered the charts in April 1965, just after promotion to Division One had been clinched with a 4-1 win at Bury? Three months later the Fab Four offered *Help!*, while their other No 1 hit that year brought the double helping of *Day Tripper* (how appropriate) and the optimistically titled *We Can Work It Out* (oh no we can't!).

There is one final piece of overwhelming, some would say damning evidence, that the Beatles were prepared to doff their caps in deference to the Cobblers' 1960s achievement. A topsy-turvy decade completed its journey on 29 April 1969, when the side drew 1-1 at Oldham, confirming relegation back to Division Four. Six days earlier The Beatles had gone to No 1 with *Get Back*.

I rest my case. And perhaps one day we will.

CHAPTER ONE

FOUNDATIONS AND FIFTIES

To most of the footballing nation, the name Herbert Chapman simply represents an Arsenal legend, a man who shaped the game after the First World War. That though, would be to denigrate all his other achievements with Huddersfield Town, Leeds City ... and of course Northampton Town.

Fame by association. After a while you come to realise that Northampton is quite spectacular in this field. For Dave Bowen, an Arsenal player for nine years in the 1950s, and the man responsible for the Cobblers footballing 'miracle', followed an almost direct line of descendancy in football management from Chapman himself.

So really, when Bowen took charge at the County Ground as player-manager in 1959, it was perfectly obvious (!) that something dramatic was about to happen. Ignore the form-book, which merely said that in 31 seasons of Division Three (South) football since its formation in 1920-21 the Cobblers had never been promoted. Only the champions went up in those days, and while filling the runners-up spot in 1927-28 (behind Millwall) and 1949-50 (Notts County) were stout efforts (also third places in 1928-29 and 1952-53), they didn't alter the equilibrium.

Such inertia is always a little frustrating, even if the long wait for something dramatic to happen makes it more spectacular when it actually does. Some would say all of this is typical of Northampton over the years, somewhere 'stuck' at a mid-point just off the M1 between London and Birmingham. A nearly town. Presumably, somebody somewhere made a great deal of money in a shady unlicensed betting shop at the end of the Division Three (North-South) divide in 1958, when the improved transport network in the country helped smooth the passage to create Division Three and Division Four.

In which division would Northampton start their new life? The clever money said that 'nondescript Northampton', as they were later cruelly dubbed in a national newspaper, would finish season 1957-58 in thirteenth place, thereby missing out on a place in the new Division Three by one position, thus playing in Division Four.

And so it came to pass ... a late-season run of seven wins and a draw from nine games ending with back-to-back defeats by Southend. When the final whistle blew at Roots Hall on 2 May 1958, the scoreline Southend 6 Northampton 3 confirmed it would be football's basement, from that fated thirteenth position. Doubtless, Herbert Chapman would have spent a few restless hours turning in his grave.

Chapman had become manager of Northampton in 1907, enjoying his first success in 1909-10 when the club won the Southern League Championship. After returning to his native Yorkshire to manage Leeds City in 1912, his prestige began to seriously shake up the old order and he then joined Huddersfield Town, firstly as assistant manager, becoming manager in September 1920.

Within two years The Terriers had captured the FA Cup which they had narrowly failed to lift in Chapman's first year (losing to Aston Villa), beating Preston 1-0. Chapman went on to win two league championships with Huddersfield but had left for Arsenal before they reeled off their hat-trick in 1926.

At Arsenal, Chapman turned around a becalmed ship to achieve the sort of dominance of which, in later years, Bertie Mee and Arsene Wenger would have been proud. Runners-up to Huddersfield in the 1926 championship, Chapman was at Wembley the following year (losing 0-1 to Cardiff) before winning the FA Cup in 1930, where the 2-0 victims were Huddersfield.

Chapman's life was cut short at the age of 55 in 1934 which meant he failed to see the culmination of all that he put in place. Arsenal won their first championship under his steering hand in 1931 and after Everton briefly gatecrashed the party the next year, the Gunners took the title for the next three seasons. His legacy is sustained today. No wonder his marble bust is so revered in the entrance hall of Highbury's main stand.

Bowen, who was born in Maesteg on 7 June 1928, was just six years old when Chapman passed away, but the link between the two men was Tom Whittaker, Chapman's trainer and later an Arsenal manager in his own right.

It was Whittaker who acted on the recommendation of his son Pat, who had spotted Bowen's potential during their time together in the RAF. As a boy at Maesteg Grammar School, Bowen had played rugby with Glyn Davies, a future Welsh international, as well as cricket with Bernard Hughes, who went on to play for Glamorgan. Football though, was the sport where Bowen would truly make his mark, although one story from his youth relates how Bowen contracted rheumatic fever to briefly raise fears that he would never play active sport again. Only by winning a pair of football boots in a raffle, the story goes, did he acquire the impetus to start again.

Bowen's departure from Northampton for the bright city lights ironically coincided with one of the Cobblers' more vibrant spells under manager Bob Dennison, who ran team affairs from March 1949 until July 1954. He then managed Middlesbrough for nine years, where he will always be remembered for signing a young Brian Clough.

When passing your eye down the long list of Northampton managers it is easy to overlook Dennison's contribution to the club, when compared with Chapman and Bowen and in later years Graham Carr and Ian Atkins, who all won promotions and trophies.

Born in Amble, Northumberland in 1912, Dennison started his career as an inside-forward for Newcastle before playing for Nottingham Forest and Fulham. He guested for the Cobblers as a player during the war years, having by now adapted his game, becoming a centre-half.

His strengths were his natural sense of leadership and a strong character, which demanded respect. After succeeding Tom Smith, Dennison guided the Cobblers to a top-five finish in Division Three (South) on three occasions, not to mention exciting FA Cup runs. When he left the club, chairman Eric Hawtin ruefully admitted: 'We have lost a great friend and a man who has done a great amount for this club.'

In 1949-50 Dennison inspired progress to the fifth round of the Cup, before the Cobblers were beaten 2-4 at Derby in front of a crowd of 38,063. That landmark was reached after a sequence which included victories over Walthamstow Avenue (4-1), Torquay (4-2), Southampton (3-2 at The Dell in a replay after a 1-1 draw at the County Ground watched by a crowd of 23,209), and Bournemouth (2-1 at the County Ground in another mid-week afternoon return in front of 22,644).

Sidney Cann's Southampton were in Division Two but the Cobblers triumphed after a goalless first half, thanks to goals by Arthur Dixon, Gwyn Hughes and Maurice Candlin. In the Saints side was Charlie Wayman who four seasons later would score in every round of the competition for Preston, including the final, when they were beaten 2-3 by West Brom.

In the fourth round, Jack English and Adam McCulloch scored the goals to knock out Bournemouth, a win which was only achieved after Cherries' full-back Ian Drummond had his leg broken by Tom Smalley, who had performed a similarly dubious act on the Saints' winger Ernie Jones in the first match with Southampton.

The effect of the FA Cup run was startling. One thing is for sure. Factories in the town had a quiet afternoon on the day of the Bournemouth replay, while there were cases of boys being expelled from the nearby Northampton Grammar School by headmaster 'Stinger' Nettleton, once it was proven that the only fever they had contracted was the contagious type, caused by close proximity to the FA Cup.

The dream died dramatically at Derby, where the issue was virtually settled by the Cobblers going 0-3 down in the first seventeen minutes. Dixon pulled one back, but it was 1-4 at half-time and Dixon's second only served to make the scoreline a little more respectable.

The Cobblers finished runners-up to Notts County in the league that season, playing the champions twice in three days at end of April, by which point County were already promoted. They had clinched that honour in their previous match with a 2-0 win over local rivals Nottingham Forest, courtesy of goals by their legendary England centre-forward Tommy Lawton and Jackie Sewell.

Eric Houghton's County also won 2-0 in an evening game against the Cobblers. Lawton, who later came to Northamptonshire to manage Kettering for two spells, hit both the goals, but the Cobblers triumphed 5-1 in the return, thanks to doubles from Dixon and Bert Mitchell and one by Arch Garrett.

That County side not only boasted Lawton and Sewell, but also England internationals Frank Broome and Leon Leuty. It was no mean effort from Dennison's side to get to within seven points of them.

Ben Collins had been born and raised in the village of Kislingbury, which modern day visitors to Northampton pass on the approach from Junction 16 of the M1. Like Bowen, he was born in 1928 and his name was to become synonymous with the Welshman through the 'Bowen and Collins' Sports shop, which they jointly owned for some years in Northampton's Gold Street, until Bowen relinquished his interest and it simply became 'Collins Sports'.

In April 1950, Collins was a raw 22-year-old centre-half with just a handful of first-team appearances behind him. Yet he was asked to mark Lawton in both matches, a daunting prospect for a young man in awe of a footballing hero.

'He took the trouble to find out my Christian name and was a real gentleman,' said Collins. 'He spoke to me all through the match. I remember jumping with him for a corner and my head was only against his waist because he rose so far. His header was just a quiet flick and it flew past the upright of the post. The other thing I remember about him was his immaculate hairstyle, all plastered down.'

Lawton's inspiration to Collins meant that when he was dropped off by the team coach on the outskirts of Kislingbury, he trotted back into the village practising his heading technique to improve his suspected weak area: 'Every fifty yards or so there was a telegraph pole and each time I reached one I would jump in the air,' he said. 'Anyone who saw me that night would have thought I was crackers!'

One of the memorable characters from that season was Eddie 'Spud' Murphy, a skilful inside-forward who had scored the winner for Morton in the 1948 Scottish FA Cup semi-final against Celtic, before playing in both matches against Rangers at Hampden Park in front of a crowd total of 265,000 (Rangers winning the replay 1-0).

Murphy was signed by Morton from Hibernian just in time for the semi-final and struck the only goal in the second period of extra-time. A 1948 souvenir album dedicated to the Cappielow club described it as: 'no fluke goal or a scrappy effort caused by a defensive lapse but the outcome of quick thinking and excellent opportunism of Greenock's new chum. Murphy hit the ball from about fourteen yards out when the leather was about a foot from the ground and Celtic's keeper, Willie Miller, touched it but failed to keep out this raking drive.'

I have to declare a vested interest here. When Murphy, who scored thirteen goals during the 1949-50 season, first came to Northampton, he stayed in digs on Bushland Road with my second cousin Michael and his parents, Bert and Millie. If you are asking yourself what a man who had graced a Scottish Cup final was doing just over a year later weaving his magic in Division Three (South), it appears the Morton stars of 1947-48 quickly 'lost the plot' and were relegated the following season. Murphy himself had something of a reputation for going off the rails.

The tale I like to recall is one of Murphy's first Sunday morning appearance at the Beesley breakfast table, looking somewhat the worse for wear, having spent much of the night in the front garden. It appears he was instantly caught in a verbal crossfire, not helped when he requested coffee (which was scarce in Northampton suburbia in the late 1940s). 'Mr Murphy, I would ask that as long as you stay under this roof, you never come home in this sort of state again,' Millie is purported to have admonished (I can almost see her wagging her finger). And as Michael remarked some years later: 'And to be fair, he never did that again. Some nights though, he never came home at all!'

Murphy's talent was wayward. He and rugged Jarrow-born Maurice Candlin, who the Cobblers signed from Partick Thistle at the same time – over the summer of 1949 – were prone to mischief which would have taken all of Dennison's man-management to control. On Christmas Day 1950 the Cobblers drew 0-0 at Crystal Palace. Murphy purloined a team-mate's bottle of beer which he had saved for the return journey, but had been foolhardy enough to publicise on the trip down. There was uproar on the coach when the theft was discovered.

Season 1950-51 brought bitter disappointment in the league, a situation rescued by an heroic 2-3 fourth round FA Cup defeat at the holders

Arsenal, after a 3-1 success at home to Barnsley – who included Danny Blanchflower – in the previous round. Murphy was instrumental in that win, firing an English cross into the net before a mesmerising dribble ten minutes from time allowed Bert Mitchell to make it 2-0. Barnsley immediately pulled a goal back, only for Mitchell to add his second from the penalty-spot after Adam McCulloch had been fouled.

The appointment with Tom Whittaker's Arsenal was assured when the Gunners won a replay 4-1 at Carlisle, but Murphy was missing from the team which faced a crowd of 72,408. That remains the biggest post-war gate at Highbury, and is partly attributable to the Gunners being hell-bent on retaining the Cup they had clinched the previous season with a 2-0 win over Liverpool.

Jack English scored both Cobblers goals on a day when centre-half Ted Duckhouse was injured in the opening minutes and spent almost the entire game limping at inside-forward. Heroes sometimes leap from unlikely quarters, and with the seconds ticking away Duckhouse set off on a surging run, shrugging off tackles as he went. The one-time Birmingham player finally unleashed a ferocious shot from twenty yards which cannoned off the crossbar. The whistle blew, and the Cobblers were out of the FA Cup.

The fact that Murphy had almost single-handedly destroyed Angus Seed's Barnsley with his flicks and passes proved significant in March 1951 when he signed for the Yorkshire club, which paid out a then record fee of £8,000. Barnsley were flush from the sale of Blanchflower to Aston Villa, and Murphy was present with Dennison, Murphy, Seed and Barnsley chairman Joe Richards at a Birmingham hotel when the deals were signed and dated.

The bizarre twist to this tale was that Richards had not intended the players to eat at the table he had booked. While Dennison insisted that Murphy partake, Blanchflower was left outside in a car, eating sandwiches with the chauffeur. The Barnsley chairman, who was knighted for his services to football and later became President of the Football League, had earned the reputation of being a 'tightwad' who rarely paid money for transfers on players unless it was instantly recouped.

How's this for a footballing trivia question? 'What was significant about Northampton Town's 2-3 home defeat by Walsall on 15 March 1957?' The answer goes a long way towards unveiling the club's key figure of the 1950s.

Study the team sheet for that game and you will find no record of one Tommy 'Flash' Fowler. His customary No 11 shirt was taken that day by

Hugh Morrow. But as that was the only game Fowler missed for five seasons – from the start of 1952-53 – we have to accept that everyone deserves a 'day off' every now and then. That player's significance over a fifteen-year period spanned three different decades. But for the war, his career would surely have been even more pronounced.

Fowler remains Northampton's record appearance maker, and the chances of any modern player racking up his tally of 552 league and cup matches (521 in the league), laced with 88 goals (84 league) seems remote. His partnership with Jack English, who remains the club's record all-time goalscorer (143), was fruitful during the late 1940s and almost the entire decade which followed.

Fowler, born in Prescot on Merseyside, had been on the books at Everton before the war, but made his official Northampton debut in the opening Division Three (South) fixture in peacetime. That was a 4-1 home win over Swindon on 31 August 1946. Fowler's first goals (two) came three weeks later in a 3-2 win at Norwich.

Fowler might have enjoyed a remarkable career at outside-left, but it nearly didn't happen. Years after he pulled off a Cobblers shirt for the last time, following a 2-2 draw with Lincoln on 9 September 1961, he was still proud to show his British Army helmet with two bullet holes. The shot came in and went out, thanks to the sniper fire which almost claimed his life at Normandy in 1944.

'The bullet just grazed my head – I was lucky,' he recalled. 'I was in a crouching position. If I had been standing I wouldn't have had a football career.'

The happy goalscoring knack which developed between Fowler and English – the winger delivering the service with his runs and crosses to the far post, and the other ghosting in to plant headers past despairing goalkeepers – proved a constant source of goals, with 'Gentleman Jack's' career extending into Bowen's early spell of player-management, and Fowler's just a little longer.

The pair's uncanny understanding was not something they practised in training. 'It was just automatic,' said Fowler. 'I knew where he was going to be and I didn't have to look up. You didn't know how he had got away from his marker but I think it was because he was so quick. He was the same type of player as Jimmy Greaves. Greaves never did a lot of chasing about – he was a goal poacher. 'Jack was fragile but he didn't half take some knocking about from full-backs. They could kick you all over the place in those days and never get a booking.'

Playing alongside this duo in the Cobblers side between 1951 and 1954 was the nimble and lethal Freddie Ramscar, whose 59 goals in 146 appearances further served to supplement English and Fowler's exploits. An unlikely looking hero, Ramscar always seemed thin on top, but played football with a shrewdness few around him could match.

The most famous story about Ramscar concerns the first match after his transfer to Millwall. He was permitted to travel to The Den on the Northampton coach and then had the cheek to score the winning goal for Millwall. History does not record whether his seat was still available on the way home.

Theo Foley's first contact with the Cobblers was as an Exeter City player in direct opposition to Fowler. Foley had signed for Exeter in 1955, having initially arrived on these shores from Dublin's Home Farm club in his native Ireland to join Burnley.

Curiously, the man who would proudly lead out the Cobblers at Everton in Division One ten years later was beginning at St James' Park in Devon at the time Eddie Murphy's professional career was winding down. Murphy had signed for the Grecians from Barnsley for a small fee, the deal being completed by an ex-Cobblers player – and at that time Exeter manager – Norman Dodgin.

Foley recalled: 'When I went to Exeter I stayed in the same digs which Eddie had once used with a wonderful lady called Mrs Huxham. By that time he had married Cynthia and they had a family together. Eddie was a bit of a boy and I remember the old-fashioned wardrobe in the bedroom which had a boot in the corner where you could put shoes and where Eddie kept his whisky bottles! He was only small and he had terrific guile but you wouldn't want to cross him as he could be nasty and give you a "smack".'

Foley's clashes with the nifty Fowler were guaranteed to be awkward affairs, and Foley admitted: 'Tommy Fowler was a horrible player to come up against, if a lovely bloke. He had a beautiful left foot and struck up a terrific rapport with Jack English, whose father had been manager at both Exeter and Northampton.'

Given that Foley was present for the Grecians' 0-9 hammering by the Cobblers at the County Ground, on 12 April 1958, his assessment of Fowler is hardly eyebrow-raising. That victory arrived three months after the famous 3-1 FA Cup triumph over Arsenal. While both wins were memorable to Cobblers fans, the magic of the Cup victory over Jack Crayston's side, boasting a half-back line of Cliff Holton, Dave Bowen and Bill Dodgin – all to later play major roles at Northampton – will always hold greater sway.

Bobby Tebbutt, born in the Northamptonshire town of Irchester – which would produce the Liverpool and England defender Phil Neal –

was an integral figure in both matches. Tebbutt only played in the third round Arsenal Cup-tie on 4 January after Alan Woan called off with blood poisoning. Woan was banned from the ground that week in case his rash proved to be contagious, but he might have heard the roars from his Abington Avenue flat, yards from the County Ground. Tebbutt was among the goalscorers, along with Ken Leek and Barry Hawkings.

In the mauling of Exeter, both Tebbutt and Woan scored hat-tricks, while there were also goals for Roly Mills (two) and one by Hawkings. Two weeks earlier the Cobblers had thrashed Millwall 7-2, so goals were not in short supply at that time.

Town's manager at this time of the Cup giant-killing was Dave Smith, who had succeeded Dennison, and Smith was understandably euphoric: 'They can't keep us out of the history books now,' he remarked. The result triggered memories of Arsenal's FA Cup defeat at the hands of Walsall 25 years earlier and the Cobblers 2-0 giant-killing at Huddersfield in the fourth round a year later, in 1934.

It might all have been different had a shot by Scottish international David Herd gone in instead of hitting a post at 1-1, but when Hawkings cheekily hooked the ball over his own shoulder to score on the hour, followed by his cross being cleared into Leek's path with fourteen minutes left, the writing was on the wall.

Reaction was overwhelming. A magnanimous Bowen, who skippered Arsenal that day, cemented local friendships by relaying his thoughts on the local hospital radio. Bowen accepted that Smith's side had deserved their victory. Cobblers skipper Ron Patterson, who had been with the club since arriving from Middlesbrough in 1952, said: 'We felt better as the game went on,' adding, 'the crowd's enthusiasm and cheering was worth a goal to us.' Crayston entered the Cobblers' dressing room after the game to congratulate his team's conquerors and join them in a celebratory glass of champagne.

The fourth round took Dave Smith's side to a snowbound Liverpool, who had needed two matches to dispose of Southend from the Cobblers' own division in round three. Smith himself watched Liverpool lose at home to Middlesbrough on the previous Saturday. Four days' preparation in the frozen wastes of Southport, including bracing spells on the beach, failed to deliver the dream as the Cobblers went down 1-3.

Two days before the game, four inches of snow blanketed the Anfield pitch and, across the city, Everton's tie with Blackburn fell victim to the weather. The uncertainty didn't deter some 6,000 fans travelling from Northampton, many of them on board nine train 'specials' laid on for the occasion from the town's Castle Station and nearby Wellingborough.

Part of the players' preparations involved the traditional Cup 'potion'. When the side departed on the Tuesday, five dozen carefully packed eggs from the farm of vice-chairman Wally Penn went with them. Added to sherry, glucose and orange juice, the potent mix, taken on the eve of each tie, had helped account for Newport, Bournemouth and Arsenal, even if it had caused mirth and provided material for music hall comedians of the time. Would Liverpool be left with egg on their faces?

With Hawkings again on the scoresheet for Northampton, cancelling out Billy Liddell's 28th-minute opener, anything seemed possible. With eleven minutes left there was still the chance of an upset. Then came Ben Collins' moment of destiny, as the Cobblers' centre-half planted a header past his own goalkeeper, Reg Elvy, in front of a mightily relieved Kop. Louis Bimpson added a third for Liverpool three minutes later. For years afterwards Collins lived with his dread moment, admitting: 'You have to be remembered for something and it is only human nature that my own goal should stick in their minds. One day a fellow brought his son into my shop, pointed at me and said: "There's the man who headed an own goal in front of the Kop at Liverpool".'

If the Cobblers' defeat at Liverpool was an anticlimax, the FA Cup rug was pulled more firmly from under their feet the following season, when they were beaten 1-2 at amateurs Tooting & Mitcham in the second round, having disposed of Wycombe at the first hurdle. Tooting had already defeated Bournemouth, and it was scant consolation that they drew with eventual winners Nottingham Forest in the third round, before losing the replay.

While this was the first 'Division Four' campaign, it was the last one under Smith, and the Cobblers were like lightning off the blocks. Woan, whose son Ian later enjoyed stardom for Nottingham Forest, had the distinction of scoring the first ever goal in Division Four in the first minute at Port Vale, when the Cobblers won 4-1 against the eventual champions.

Indeed, the first five matches were won, but the side could ultimately finish only eighth, despite Woan top scoring with 32 league goals, a figure only shadowed since by the 36 which Cliff Holton bagged three seasons later.

Woan lasted just a few months into the Bowen era, as the new player-manager began his 'revolving door' policy with forwards, a habit to which he would rigidly adhere during the rise to Division One. In this instance, it was Crystal Palace who offered cash and the forward Mike Deakin in a deal which sent Woan to Selhurst Park.

Given the signs that Bowen was intent on shuffling his forwards with more dexterity than the average East End card shark, it is not surprising that we have to look elsewhere when pinning down the first league appearance of a Cobbler destined to perform in Division One.

With that glorious gift of hindsight, there are several good reasons to take special interest in the Cobblers' 4-3 win at Exeter on 28 February 1959. For one thing, Theo Foley was still biding his time in the Exeter side, still waiting for a move he would make in May 1961; for another, Dave Smith's side were moving confidently up the table; and most significantly of all, Derek Leck made a goalscoring debut. Leck, in fact, was playing in attack at Exeter, but Bowen would later re-model the Deal-born player as an attacking wing-half, which was probably the reason he managed to stay at the club so long.

Leck recalls: 'The ball was played through and I was still in my own half. I looked across at the linesman who waved "go on" and I was left one on one with the goalkeeper. An Exeter player thumped into the back of me but at the last second I moved to the right and lifted the ball over the goalkeeper.'

It was an encouraging start for Leck, who had bided his time since joining Northampton in a deal struck eight months earlier with Dave Smith on Euston Station. His eight games for Millwall had seen him score on his first two outings in 1957-58 – a 3-0 victory over Crystal Palace, which brought the headline: 'Leck lights up the Old Kent Road', and a 2-1 win over Port Vale.

Early goals for new clubs might have been a trademark to his career, as his home Cobblers debut brought two goals in a 4-0 win over Coventry but it wasn't something he achieved when he moved to his final league club, Brighton, in November 1965 … even though they crushed Southend 9-1.

Bowen arrived in the summer of 1959 to take over from Smith as player-manager, and his first season in charge was one of acclimatisation. Other than Leck, none of the Division One players would surface during his first campaign.

Despite living in Cockfosters in North London and having teammates Jimmy Bloomfield and Tommy Docherty as neighbours, Bowen had retained his Northampton links and even trained with the Cobblers on occasions – although this was banned prior to the 1958 FA Cup-tie.

Bowen's Arsenal and Welsh experience had served a more than useful purpose, creating a network of national and international contacts. While the Northampton budget would ultimately restrict him, there was plenty of free rein with which to begin.

CHAPTER TWO

THE ONLY WAY IS UP

The coming of the 1960s changed everything for Northampton Town. Precisely five years, three months and 21 days after kicking of the '60s at home to Doncaster, the Cobblers were concluding the most successful season in their history, and making plans for Division One. In those five and a half seasons, 123 of their 245 league matches had been won, another 58 drawn, and just 64 lost. In that time they averaged nearly two goals a game, scoring on 460 occasions and conceding 317.

It seems Northampton couldn't wait to cast aside the shackles of the 1950s, but even Dave Bowen did not work an instant miracle. In 1959-60, the second season of the new Division Four – and his first as player-manager – the club finished sixth, only fading from the promotion picture in the final two matches.

Bobby Tebbutt – one of the goalscoring heroes of the 1958 FA Cup win over Arsenal – not only scored the last Cobblers goal of the 1950s, in a 2-1 home defeat by Watford on 28 December, but also netted the first of the '60s against Rovers. But Tebbutt's league career was destined to end at Walsall in the March, when his right leg was broken. The clock was moving forwards, not back.

Christmas 1959 saw the Cobblers struggling in the bottom seven in Division Four. The Boxing Day match at Watford at least brought temporary respite as, trailing to a Cliff Holton penalty after Colin Gale fouled Dennis Uphill, the game was abandoned after fifty minutes. The headline in Northampton's evening newspaper, *The Chronicle & Echo*, screamed out: 'WATFORD PITCH BECAME JUST A SEA OF WATER.'

Two days later, that man Uphill – who scored goals for all six of his league clubs, the others being Tottenham, Reading, Coventry, Mansfield and Crystal Palace – bagged two inside a minute. They ensured that Tebbutt's late penalty was no more than a consolation.

Perhaps the most interesting other feature of the match was a black and white dog joining the Cobblers defence at 0-0, only to be delicately carried off by Gale, whose general ruggedness and thickness of neck gave him the nickname 'horse' among supporters.

As the 1960s peeped around the curtains in Northamptonshire, the local *Chronicle & Echo* ran a story which reflected progress of a kind, the closing of the branch railway line between Northampton and Market Harborough as part of an economy drive by the British Transport

Commission. Except that reporter Gordon Harmer and photographer Bob Price found themselves reporting on the 'engine that died of shame', No 41218, a sister locomotive to the Class Two passenger engine. Earlier on the Saturday evening it had smoothly operated the final run of the 'push and pull' service between Northampton and nearby Blisworth, but had now broken down, stranding joy-riding passengers for nearly an hour until a replacement could be brought into service. Progress of any kind it seemed, be it on the railway or at the football club, would not be easy around these parts.

Three months without a home win is taking the fasting business a little bit too far though, and the Cobblers were about to turn a corner. On 2 January 1960 you needed a fair memory to recall the 2-0 success over Aldershot on 3 October 1959, earned with goals by Leck and Woan. Six home matches and a change of decade later, the portents were not immediately brighter.

For one thing, football was not the No 1 attraction in a town which had a population of 100,300 inside the borough, while the county registered some 388,600. Northampton and England scrum-half Dickie Jeeps was the town's Sportsman of the Year, and for entertainment, there were queues to see Leslie Caron, Maurice Chevalier and Louis Jordan in *Gigi* at the Essoldo, *North By NorthWest* at the Gaumont, John Paul Jones at the Savoy, *North West Frontier* at the Ritz, and the *Gladiators* at the Plaza. Doncaster Rovers, one of just six clubs below the Cobblers, and twenty away matches without a win, were not an obvious distraction when it came to spending a hard earned shilling. Some 6,253 hardy souls though, felt it was worth their while.

Flagkick, the '*Chron*'s' football correspondent, dutifully recorded that the Doncaster match kicked off ten minutes early to ensure it ended in passable light. Bowen returned to the side in the No 6 shirt, and the player-manager also recalled the former West Brom winger Frank Griffin. Griffin had scored the last-gasp winner in the 1954 FA Cup final, which defeated Preston 3-2, after which he is reported to have said: 'My heart stopped beating when I realised I scored the goal that won us the Cup.'

Griffin was 31 when he became one of Bowen's first signings from Shrewsbury, but made just seventeen appearances before drifting into non-league at Wellington. It's safe to say Northampton fans didn't see the best of him.

Against Doncaster though, Griffin made a positive impact. After Ron Walker had cancelled out Tebbutt's headed opener, Mills headed in a Griffin free-kick which goalkeeper Bill Nimmo conceded just outside his penalty area before the break, while Fowler, who had laid on Tebbutt's goal, made it 3-1 midway through the second half following a goalmouth scramble.

It's easy to be wise after the event, but the 'Club Gossip' notes for the Doncaster match programme now make the sort of reading which would send Mystic Meg scurrying into premature retirement. The Nostradamus of his day stated: 'We hope to see more successful results in the future, for, as our chairman Walter Penn stated at the club's annual general meeting before Christmas, the club is pursuing a long-term policy under Dave Bowen, with the sole purpose of taking the club into a higher sphere, and the future can be viewed with confidence. Young players are being found, and with proper coaching and training should eventually become successful first team players. In the space of four short months it is possible to see the shape of things to come, and manager Bowen is taking stock in every way to better the club as soon as possible.'

Instant prophetic stuff, when you then realise the Doncaster win was the first of sixteen in 23 matches, and with only five defeats, the Cobblers rose dramatically to sixth, twelve points behind champions Walsall and seven adrift of runners-up Notts County.

Included in that run were some spectacular efforts, an 8-1 home win over Oldham in February in which Tebbutt fired a hat-trick, with doubles for Mike Deakin and Peter Kane, while both Walsall and County were defeated in the March. April saw drubbings of Barrow (6-0), with Deakin hitting four and Kane a brace, and Southport away (4-0), a match in which Kane took his turn to notch a treble.

Deakin, signed from Crystal Palace in late October, was the brother of Alan, the Aston Villa and England Under-23 wing-half who would play against the Cobblers in Division One. He ended this season as top scorer with twenty goals in just 25 appearances, a return which rewarded Bowen's 'short, sharp burst' theory with forwards who were then often discarded or transferred.

In the days before footballers were regularly labelled 'versatile', it became apparent that Deakin's talents stretched beyond the football field. He had an alternative career as a plumber. A teammate recalled him fixing the loo in the freezing Hartlepool dressing room before going out to score two goals in a 4-1 on 7 November, the club's last victory of the 1950s. 'All in a day's work,' he apparently said, or words to that effect.

Peter Kane had the distinction of scoring the Cobblers' 'one' in their 1-7 first round FA Cup mauling at the hands of Torquay, with all bar one of the goals coming in the second half. The Cup exit came in the wake of a 3-5 league defeat at Plainmoor in the September. Kane also profited with sixteen goals in 28 league games, moving on to Arsenal at the end of the campaign before returning for a second spell with the Cobblers in 1963, which then triggered three productive years at Crewe.

A colourful character known as 'Kipper', Kane was a Scottish welter-weight boxing champion in 1957-58 who also laced his life with management at Barrow, when they first dropped into non-league in 1971-72. He later ran a hotel in Blackpool while providing a regular turn as a hotel-pub crooner around the North-West seaside resort.

The end of the 1959-60 campaign was also significant for Bowen, as he called 'time' on his own playing career. Bowen handed his No 6 jersey to the club's faithful servant Mills following a 0-3 February defeat at Aldershot, a side run by the former Northampton boss Dave Smith. Also playing in that match was goalkeeper Charlie 'Chic' Brodie, who would sign for Bowen a year later, while one of the goals was scored by ex-Cobbler Brian Kirkup.

In a sentimental farewell, Bowen recalled himself for the final home game of the season two months later, a goalless draw with Crewe, but the writing was on the wall and it was Mills at right-half who did most to inspire a stuttering Cobblers performance. In total, Bowen played 35 league and cup games for Northampton, either side of his 146 league appearances for Arsenal over nine years. And of course there were those nineteen Welsh caps.

Goalscoring never threatened to play a dominant part in the Bowen repertoire, but if you are going to record just four in your career, you might as well make them interesting for trivia buffs in years to come. So, when reviewing the career of David Lloyd Bowen, try this one for size. Which of the following is the odd one out? Is it: a) Tel Aviv, b) White Hart Lane, or c) Borough Park?

There isn't much that Israel and Workington have in common, but the answer is of course 'b', and the reason for this is simple. Bowen scored once during the 1958 World Cup qualifier, which his country won 2-0 (Ivor Allchurch hit the other), and once in Northampton's 1-5 thrashing at the hands of Workington in their first away match of the 1960s. But in the North London derby played out in front of 65,455 people on 13 March 1957, Bowen hit a double and Derek Tapscott the other, as Arsenal defeated Tottenham 3-1. Bowen generally left the goalscoring to others, and during his managerial career had precious few loyalties as he chopped and changed strikers.

There's a delightful irony to Bowen's one and only Cobblers goal, which arrived just before half-time at Workington. It pulled the score back to 2-1 and arrived with the assistance of home goalkeeper Malcolm Newlands, whose decision to kick rather than handle misfired, allowing the ball to apologetically trickle over the line. Newlands, incidentally, was the name of the sweet shop by Northampton Market Square, which used to be run by Bowen's mum Martha, so it has always had lucky connotations with the family.

It is a curious coincidence that the first match of 1960-61 – the season that marked the start of the Cobblers' climb – and the final game of 1968-69, when they returned to Division Four, were on the same ground. That was never going to be the County Ground, a point of which local diehards were always too painfully aware. The football club had a duty to vacate the premises on 30 April every year, to allow Northants County Cricket Club to begin their cricketing duties. On only three occasions between the end of the Second World War and 1994 – when they waved goodbye to their old home for the Sixfields Stadium – were the Cobblers at home on the opening day of the season. Those games saw wins over Swindon (4-1 in 1946-47) and Rotherham (3-1 in 1973-74), and a 1-1 draw with Scunthorpe (1981-82).

No, the pieces of string which neatly tied together both ends of the roller-coaster years were pulled tight at Oldham's Boundary Park. The great ascent began on one of the highest grounds in the country on 20 August 1960. Eight years, eight months and 397 league matches later, it ended there with a 1-1 draw which confirmed the club's relegation to Division Four. Sandwiched in the middle was an almighty adventure.

Let's be honest, if you are going to spend nine years stretching the limits of credibility, where better to start than Boundary Park, especially if your own home ground doubles up as a cricket pitch. The cricket presented a problem almost unique to the Cobblers, with Sheffield United's Bramall Lane the only realistic comparison.

Inevitably, there were often periods in late April and August when the crossover period could be extremely thin and hurried for groundstaff and their helpers. In early May, it is doubtful whether white-flannelled outfielders preparing to collect and throw in a speeding cricket ball would be greatly encouraged to know that only days before, the studs of a flying left-winger attacking the Hotel End, not to mention his covering full-back, were digging into that very turf.

When the Cobblers made their home Division One bow on a Wednesday evening against Arsenal in 1965, Northants CCC had been on the threshold of a first ever County Championship win 24 hours earlier. On the Monday, the county's legendary England batsman Colin Milburn had flayed the Gloucestershire attack for a memorable unbeaten 152 as Northants declared on 227-5. Declarations and interruptions for rain failed to bring a result, and with Northants' campaign completed, they had to sit back and wait as Worcestershire overhauled their points total with matches in hand. Northants are still awaiting their first title.

Cobblers striker Bobby Hunt recalled watching some of the cricket action unfold with a sense of disbelief, knowing that Division One football would be played on the next evening. Talk about enforcing the follow on!

The Bowen side which kicked off 1960-61 with a 2-1 victory – courtesy of a double by Deakin – lined up: Brewer, Claypole, Patterson, Cooke, Gale, Mills, Tucker, Deakin, Laird, Wright, Fowler. Not one of those men were to play in Division One, although Leck was back in the side four days later in the 0-3 defeat at Workington, and by the end of the campaign, names such as Terry Branston, Norman Coe, Mike Everitt and Barry Lines were stirring in the consciousness of supporters.

The Oldham match might serve now as a landmark, but in truth it hardly set the pulses racing at the time. Cobblers supporters rushing out to buy the No 1 record in the charts at the time – Cliff Richard and *Please Don't Tease* – could well have had their football club in mind. Oldham had needed to apply for re-election the previous season (above only Hartlepool) and although their new manager, Jack Rowley, included among his new signings Morton's Jimmy Frizzell, who would later manage the club, the Latics' improvement that term meant a modest twelfth place.

Deakin put the visitors ahead after 75 minutes but Peter Stringfellow equalised. But for Kevin McCurley being forced off injured on his Oldham debut after signing from Colchester (never to play in the league again), it is unlikely both points would have been won. As it was, Deakin hit a last-minute winner. New *Chronicle & Echo* correspondent Dave Jones was therefore regarded as something of a lucky talisman and afterwards wrote: 'The Cobblers will play far better than this and lose.'

But not too often … The Workington defeat that followed triggered a run of eight consecutive league victories. This ended in another remote North-West outpost, Barrow, and the Cobblers went into their long-awaited first ever local derby at Peterborough, on 8 October, searching for a first victory in four games.

The London Road club had fought long and hard to earn a place in the Football League on the back of a string of Midland League titles, yet had been denied by the 'closed shop' network. FA Cup exploits had been rife, examples including a 1955-56 triumph over Ipswich, and a 5-4 extra-time third round replay success at Lincoln the following season, before going out 1-3 at Bill Shankly's Huddersfield, a match in which a youthful Denis Law was on target for the Terriers.

In 1959-60, Jimmy Hagan's Posh had gone out in the fourth round, losing 0-2 at Sheffield Wednesday after victories over Shrewsbury (4-3), Walsall (3-2 away), and Alf Ramsey's Ipswich (3-2 away).

If anything could temper the euphoria of a Cobblers promotion season in years to come, it would be the thought of going up, but behind Peterborough as champions. In 1960-61, this is exactly what happened. Posh stormed to the Division Four title, shattering the League record of 128 points in the process. When they hammered Barrow 6-2 in their final match of the season, the team had scored a remarkable 134 goals, Terry Bly accounting for 52 of them.

The first meeting between Posh and the Cobblers was a thriller, and one in which Rugby-born centre-half Branston made his debut. The Cobblers raced into a 3-0 lead at half-time thanks to goals by Deakin, Fowler and Leck. Fowler went off injured in the second half and Posh salvaged a point with Peter McNamee hitting a double and Dennis Emery the other.

The return match at the County Ground on 25 February saw a 3-0 win for the champions-elect on a mud-bath of a pitch. Everitt made a promising Cobblers debut in attack after arriving from Arsenal, but the home team were undone by Peterborough's more direct approach. Posh clinched victory thanks to a 25th-minute goal by Bly, a McNamee strike on the hour, and Ray Smith's killer twelve minutes from time

Despite flourishing somewhat in the Posh shadow, Bowen's first promotion was a decisive, well-earned affair and one which set great store for the future.

Like Branston, Barry Lines made his league debut in a contest where the Cobblers threw away a 0-3 lead, in this case in the home game with Hartlepool in November. The Bletchley teenager had been given a taste of first-team life in the League Cup replay defeat at Wrexham, the ground on which goalkeeper Norman Coe cut his teeth in a 2-2 league draw on 19 November.

After Deakin's early flourish, he was sold to Aldershot, whereupon the bulk of the goals were provided by County Durham-born Laurie Brown, who ended the season as top scorer with 25. Brown was an England amateur international who played most of his career at centre-half, but Bowen used him mostly in attack before selling him to Arsenal at the end of that season.

Brown was inspired by the responsibility of captaincy, and his haul of goals was helped in no small part by taking penalties. These were profligate around a busy Easter period, which did no great credit to those responsible for the fixture planning at Football League headquarters.

Easter began with the players watching promotion rivals York beat Hartlepool 4-0 on Good Friday before continuing their journey to meet 'Pool the following day. There, Brown missed a penalty and Hartlepool scored two as the Cobblers were beaten 2-4.

The logic of playing at Exeter on Easter Monday has disappeared into the fog of history, but it was at St James' Park that Brown stroked home a penalty, and Exeter were beaten 3-1. One more day, and two more penalties later, Exeter had been sent packing from the County Ground on the back of an identical scoreline.

The postscript to the match is that Bowen signed Exeter's Foley a month later, in readiness for the 1961-62 season. At one point in the game Everitt and Foley traded fouls, leaving the Northampton man sprawled in the penalty area. In running onto the pitch to treat his player, the story goes that Cobblers trainer Jack Jennings took a circular detour to pour words into the Exeter defender's ear. Whether Jennings was offering Foley terms is unsure, but clearly Bowen had seen something he liked.

A defeat at Carlisle and a draw at Stockport only delayed promotion, which was clinched with two games to go in the 5-1 win over Rochdale on 22 April. It was a match in which former Leicester and Norwich striker Jimmy Moran, signed from the Canaries in January, scored a second half hat-trick inside fourteen minutes.

So many strikers, and so little time. The final home game was destined to be the last Cobblers match with Accrington Stanley, before that club folded the following season. The Cobblers won 2-1, with goals from Brown and Lines, but it's intriguing to note the name of the man who fired Accrington in front. A certain George Hudson would appear on this stage much later on.

The names of Cliff Holton, Alec Ashworth and Frank Large are etched in Northampton footballing folklore. Renowned goalscorers all, and each competed in Division One, if not for the Cobblers.

Holton, who hit the target regularly for all six of his league clubs, was something of a veteran by the time he arrived at the County Ground at the age of 32 in September 1961. His arrival was a triumph for Bowen's North London contacts as Northampton was the only club Holton represented outside of the capital (if we include two spells with Watford), so Bowen achieved something special by levering him away from his other business interests.

Holton had made nearly 200 league appearances for Arsenal and played in the 1952 FA Cup final 0-1 defeat by Newcastle. That was the match in which the Gunners fell to a late goal by George Robledo and battled for over an hour with ten men after an injury to Welsh international full-back Wally Barnes.

Holton's reputation in front of the net was already remarkable. He had fired 42 goals for Watford in 1959-60 to help them to promotion from Division Four, and 32 the following year, having cost Watford £10,000 when arriving from Highbury in October 1958. Almost three years later the Cobblers paid £7,000 for his services and to say his arrival made an instant impression would be an understatement.

The scene was perfectly set for Holton. The Cobblers had failed to score in their first four matches of that 1961-62 season, and although in the fifth Pat Terry had quickly cancelled out Bert Llewellyn's early opener for Port Vale at the County Ground, Bowen's men had only two points to show from their first five matches.

The Cobblers were due at unbeaten Crystal Palace four days later on the Wednesday evening, and although the evening newspapers spoke of Holton's possible arrival, nothing had been finalised. 'Negotiations were proceeding this morning and it was hoped to finalise the deal when the Cobblers stopped for tea at Kenton on the way to the match,' read one report.

Holton did sign, and Bowen made him captain, relieving Foley of the armband. Foley is (not surprisingly) reputed to have questioned this decision, upon which Holton retorted: 'You provide the crosses, and I'll get the goals.'

Not only did Holton inspire a first victory of the season, he smashed in a hat-trick within four hours of the ink drying on his contract. While the archivists attributed the upturn in fortunes to the Cobblers' stunning past record of five wins and two draws from seven trips to Selhurst Park, most supporters quickly cottoned on to the fact that the real reason was Cliff Holton.

His Palace hat-trick was the first of four Holton delivered that season, the others coming in the 7-0 rout of Grimsby – who were amazingly promoted second behind Portsmouth – the 3-0 second round FA Cup success over Kettering (the Cobblers lost 1-3 at Port Vale in the next round), and a 4-1 victory at Notts County in April, in which Brian Etheridge made his debut. The other goal came from amateur Derek Woods, playing at outside-right.

When Holton scored two more in the 4-1 home win over Coventry, it meant he had broken the club's 33-year-old club league goalscoring record, set when Ted Bowen had racked up 34 league goals in 1928-29. Ted Bowen, like Holton and his namesake, had been another ex-Arsenal player. Holton netted in the final home game of the season (a penalty in the 1-1 draw with QPR) to take him past the 37 scored by Albert Dawes, whose 1932-33 total was bumped up by five goals in an FA Cup-tie against Lloyds.

Following the 2-0 home win over his old club Watford in December, Holton was presented with a silver salver by Hornets chairman Jim Bonser. This commemorated his feat of breaking Watford's individual scoring record in 1959-60 and being the top scorer of all English leagues, with 74 over two seasons.

It wasn't simply the volume of goals, the quality was outstanding. Holton executed a range of 30-35 yard snorting drives to break the hearts of goalkeepers, while testing the strength of football nets in his own unique nationwide survey. Roly Mills recalled Holton pulling off one such effort at Torquay to help steal an unlikely victory. Another thunderbolt went whistling in during the 2-3 defeat at Grimsby, where Holton hit a double.

Holton's reputation was such that he carried an aura of class and sophistication into the dressing room. He was a forerunner of the modern 'playboy' footballer, and would appear on match days in his smart suit with a 'pampering' bag, along with a bottle of Guinness which he would often swig before a game. Young professionals were in awe, but while he was delivering such a healthy rate of goals, nothing Holton did could be brought into question. His ability to entertain knew no bounds and at one time he and Everitt mastered a free-kick routine which was almost slapstick, as they apparently argued with one another while standing over the ball, in order to distract the opposition.

The Cobblers ended 1961-62 eighth in Division Three, with no immediate hint as to what would follow. Foley and Leck were virtual ever-presents, and Foley missed only the first round FA Cup win over Millwall. Tommy Robson was the next of the Division One crew to make his debut, at outside-left in the 2-0 win at Peterborough in March.

Season 1962-63 was a glorious one and began with Holton maintaining his rich vein of form in front of goal. The arrival of Alec Ashworth for £10,000 from Luton prompted a brief, but golden alliance with Holton before their paths diverted.

Southport-born Ashworth had begun his league career with Everton and had fired two goals on his debut for the Toffees – a 2-5 defeat by Manchester City. He also hit the target in his next game, with Blackpool. He joined Luton in October 1960 as a makeweight when Irish international Billy Bingham went the other way, and hit twenty league goals in 63 appearances for the Hatters. Among his FA Cup goals was one in the 4-0 victory over the Cobblers in 1960-61.

Ashworth had something of a 'playboy' image, and it was that side of his character which helped prompt a move from Kenilworth Road. He turned down Southampton, as a south coast switch would have left him far from his parents in Southport, and chose the Cobblers instead.

He and Holton shared 21 goals in the first ten league matches of 1962-63, one or the other being on target in each of these fixtures, which brought six wins, three draws and a total of 31 goals. Among those victories were an 8-0 mauling of Wrexham and a 7-1 thrashing of Halifax, in which Holton scored his fifth and final hat-trick for the club. The Cobblers only needed one goal to beat QPR at the County Ground in September, but it was a classic, Ashworth taking possession in the centre-circle just after half-time and embarking on a run which ended with a shot slipped past Ray Drinkwater in the Rangers goal.

Holton's final appearance before moving to Charlton was in a 1-5 defeat at Southend in December, in which Ashworth netted the consolation. Ashworth inherited the captain's mantle, but the fact that he made just ten further league appearances that season (scoring seven times to take his total for the season to 26 in league and cup) suggests that, from a goalscoring perspective, the season splits neatly into two halves, either side of that winter's big freeze.

Ashworth had emerged with credit from two League Cup-ties with Preston (who were sufficiently impressed to sign him in good time for their 1964 FA Cup final defeat by West Ham), but when the Cobblers emerged from the unscheduled 45-day winter break, there was no doubt that the key figure to emerge was Frank Large.

All championship sides need a slice of luck, and the extraordinary icy interlude came to the Cobblers' assistance, at a time when they were struggling for form. It was rather like being allowed to take a 'time-out', re-group, freshen up, and come back all the stronger.

Ashworth was sent off, along with Watford's Bob Howfield, on 27 October, in a 2-4 defeat. More significantly though, the Cobblers won only once in their next seven matches – a 2-1 win at Carlisle who were destined to be relegated with only Halifax below them.

The last of those seven games was on Boxing Day, when centre-back John Kurila was sent off in the 1-2 defeat at Notts County. In fact, as he often fondly recalled, he never served a suspension as his six-week ban coincided with the snow lying thick on the ground.

Large was watching in the crowd when the Cobblers resumed action on 9 February at QPR's White City stadium, one of just a few matches to be given the go-ahead and, for that reason, the contest was featured on *Match of the Day*.

Making his Cobblers debut was the 5ft 5ins striker Bert Llewellyn, signed from Port Vale. He broke his ankle during the match, which virtually ended his career, although he did play seventeen times in the league for Walsall during the next season.

The Cobblers beat QPR 3-1, Lines hitting a double and Ashworth netting the other. The victory was sweet for Foley. In April, at the same venue, the Cobblers' skipper had been punched by a spectator who ran across the athletics track to launch his attack, before being pinned against a goal-post by Chic Brodie.

Although the Cobblers lost 0-3 at Bournemouth a fortnight later, Large was in the Northampton side which drew 0-0 at home to Coventry on 2 March. From that point onwards, it was a case of 'Large in charge'. In the next nineteen games he scored eighteen goals, including hat-tricks at home to Colchester and Southend.

When Reading were dumped 5-0 at the County Ground on 30 March, Ashworth helped himself to a treble and Large the other two. The fact that it was Grand National day, and Ayala was romping to a 66-1 success at Aintree, helped to keep down the crowd, but the Cobblers forwards flourished thanks to the excellent wing-play of Lines and Billy Hails, who had been signed from Peterborough in December.

The Southend game was a landmark in itself, Bowen's men recording a seventh straight win in nineteen days. It was 4-2 at half-time, with Large completing his hat-trick in the 67th minute. That was the Cobblers' 100th goal of the season.

More goals were to follow as the season dragged into May, a consequence of the winter freeze. Large hit two to see off Carlisle on 9 May before the title was clinched two days later at Peterborough, who finished sixth, one place lower than twelve months earlier.

Cars tailed bumper to bumper along the A605 from Thrapston to London Road, where it was former Posh man Hails who opened the scoring midway through the first half, after a throw-in by Kurila. Jim Rayner's own-goal from a Hails cross made it 2-0 before the break. In the second half Leck floated through the home defence to flick the ball over Brian Ronson. It was Ray Smith, another former Peterborough man, who made it 4-0 two minutes from time. All that remained was for Hull City to come to the County Ground on 24 May for a grand finale, which saw the club President, Alderman CT Cripps present the championship medals to the players.

Cricket was in full swing ... Northants had beaten Warwickshire in a Knockout Cup-tie on the same ground only two days earlier, while the Hull players duly lined up to cheer the champions onto the pitch. Goals from Ashworth, John Reid and a Foley penalty set the seal on a memorable campaign, former Bradford City man Reid taking his total to eleven for the season.

If anyone thought it would be impossible to build on such euphoria, then the start of season 1963-64 did its best. It began with wins at Scunthorpe (2-1) and Sunderland (2-0) inside the space of five days in August, and when a quick double was completed over The Iron (2-0), the Division One words were already being whispered.

Bizarrely, those wins were achieved without Bowen at the helm. The Cobblers manager had apparently resigned, stating he needed a break from the game, a situation which had a precedent in September 1962 when he spent a fortnight abroad, after being ordered to take a rest. Trainer and coach Jack Jennings was left in charge on both occasions, but although former club boss Dennison was among the applicants when the job was advertised, Bowen relented and returned to his post.

The effect of all this was not immediately apparent, with the Cobblers winning only two of their next eight matches, but the season was a memorable one for all that, even if a final position of eleventh did not fulfil the early promise.

The highlight was almost certainly the 5-1 thrashing of runners-up Sunderland, on a famous afternoon when Bowen's quick-wittedness and business contacts came up trumps. The Cobblers donned baseball-style boots, bought from the Bowen & Collins Sports Shop in the town's Gold Street, and left the Wearsiders standing … or rather sliding on the frozen surface.

There were two goals that day from the teenage Don Martin, who hit seven in a season which lacked the heavy input from one outstanding striker – which had been a feature of the previous three campaigns. Frank Large topped the charts with twelve, only to set off again on his travels which would eventually play see him play for nine different clubs, when he moved to Swindon in March. He would return to Northampton in 1966 and again in 1969, eventually totting up 250 league and cup appearances and scoring 96 goals in the process.

Large was a typically bull-headed centre-forward who Northampton supporters took to their hearts. He was not the sort of man to be fazed by anything – not even a dart sticking in his back while defending a corner at Leyton Orient during a goalless draw in November 1963. The idea was simply to get on with the job. And that's exactly what Bowen and his team were doing as the steamroller chugged forward to August 1964.

CHAPTER THREE

DIVISION TWO AND RISING

It was late in August 1964, and a thick smog hung over Middlesbrough. Reporter Mike Beesley and photographer Bob Price were sitting in a brown Austin motor car overlooking the Teesside town on a Bank Holiday Monday evening. A century earlier in Dickensian London, what they were viewing might have been described as a grey 'pea-souper'. Here though, the density had a decidedly yellow hue. It all smacked of smoke and industry.

Beesley was 25 and had worked on Northampton's evening paper for nine years since leaving school, although he had served two years of National Service in the Intelligence Corps in Malaya. More accustomed to dipping into the local cinemas for film reviews, and the park bowls and cricket sporting scene, he was covering his first Cobblers league game for the *Chronicle & Echo* after taking over from Dave Jones.

The pre-season friendly at Oxford United nine days earlier had whetted his appetite. The Cobblers had drawn 2-2 with Arthur Turner's side, who would win promotion from Division Four behind Brighton, Millwall and York. It had been a good day for Cobblers 'new boys', as summer signing (from Watford) Charlie Livesey had scored in the first minute, and outside-right Harry Walden, Town's only other squad addition, had equalised after goals by Tony Jones and Colin Harrington had handed Oxford the lead.

Bob Price had been a colleague of Beesley for seven years and pointed his camera in a range of directions since moving south from his native Barrow-in-Furness. He would serve forty years on the 'Chron', leaving on 14 October 1997, the exact anniversary of his arrival.

A good-natured, ambling lover of life, Price had an oft beautiful but occasionally frustrating naivety about him. Back in 1958 he had pressed himself down in the Anfield snow at pitch-side to capture shots from the Liverpool FA Cup defeat, in order not to impede the view of spectators behind him. He at least had the sense to say 'no' when Donald Campbell had offered him a ride in his high-speed craft on Coniston Water. 'I was too scared to get on a motor-bike in those days,' he said.

Another of the stories with which Price would regale, was stopping play one Saturday morning during a Northamptonshire championship cricket match with Nottinghamshire. Having missed his bus from Mercer's Row, close to the newspaper offices, he realised his standard shot of the two opening batsmen walking down the pavilion steps would not now be possible. They were out in the middle and had made seven runs. His equipment did not cater for 'action' so he marched out onto the square to request help from the umpires.

Remarkably, they did so. The England and Northants batsman Dennis Brookes remarked 'If I'm out, I'm not out', as a ball was mocked up for him to play an 'authentic' shot which appeared in the town's *Green 'Un* sports paper that Saturday evening. History relates that Northants skipper Raman Subba Row was less than enamoured as Price returned towards the pavilion, and hailed his displeasure at some volume and length. The photographer was not unduly worried. He had his shot, even though it puzzled the sports editor Tony Rolfe. His department was granted a telephoto lens by editor Gerry Freeman the next day, so the whole business had served its purpose.

Although the town's football correspondent no longer went under the mantle of 'Flagkick' – by-lines now appearing on reports – Beesley was following an illustrious order of scribes. One of his predecessors, Maurice Ribbans, had left in 1957 to scheme the country's new motorway structure. Years later his son William would perform surgery on Michael Schumacher's broken leg after the Formula One driver's crash at nearby Silverstone. Ribbans' footballing successor, John Morris, went on to work for the *London Evening Standard* and *Sunday Express*, before returning in 1978 to run the town's sports press agency. He later became Secretary of the British Boxing Board of Control. Others, such as Jones and Don Jafkins, contributed years of loyal service to the paper, after also assuming the 'Flagkick' mantle with credit.

So, as Beesley and Price sat and debated what the new season held in store, there already existed a strong sense of 'continuing the line'.

The first league Ayresome Park programme of 1964-65 had been written before Raich Carter's side had kicked off on the Saturday with a 3-0 win at Southampton, although Boro were extolling the news that their stadium would be used as a venue during the 1966 World Cup nearly two years down the line.

Underdogs to blossom in the 1960s? For Northampton Town that year in Division Two, read North Korea in Group Four two summers on. Many of those Boro fans who witnessed Arthur Horsfield's injury-time winner that night would see the Koreans draw with Chile and then beat Italy 1-0, which (unlikely as it might sound) made Pak Doo Ik, the Korean goalscorer, a household name.

North Korea's run was destined to end in the quarter-finals in 1966 with a 3-5 defeat by Portugal, and while Northampton's momentum was slow to build, it was ultimately to prove an irresistible tide in 1964-65. Due to their age-old juggling act with the cricket club they had been idle on the opening day, when there had been mixed fortunes for newly promoted Coventry and Crystal Palace, now in Division Two. While the Sky Blues were beating Plymouth 2-0, Palace were losing 2-3 at home to Derby. Bury had fared best of all, hammering Swindon 6-1.

In Division One, Manchester United would go on to be champions but were held on the opening day, 2-2 by West Brom. Leeds and Chelsea, destined for runners-up and third spots, were winners. Don Revie's men came away from Aston Villa with a 2-1 victory, while Chelsea won at Wolves 3-0.

From the Cobblers' perspective, there would later appear a certain irony, for their scheduled opponents on that opening day were Newcastle, with whom they would fight hammer and tong for the title.

More immediately, the disappointment of the late defeat at Boro was compounded for supporters back home by the fact that the score was wrongly broadcast as a 2-1 victory on the late TV news. Beesley and Price did not arrive home until 6am.

Having lost their opener, the Cobblers collected their first points with a 2-0 win at Manchester City five days later. City paraded summer signings Dave Bacuzzi, Barry Stobart and David Connor, and had thrashed Leyton Orient 6-0 in midweek, but the Cobblers eased to victory. Next up was a quick return with Middlesbrough, who again stalled the machine on the following Tuesday.

Beesley might have been covering just his third Cobblers league game, but he was never afraid to call a match or individual performances as he saw them. When he left the *Chronicle & Echo* in the early 1970s, to spend four years on the *Nottingham Evening Post*, he did so with a remit to cover Derby County at a time when Brian Clough was bringing glory to that part of the East Midlands.

Now, Beesley took the Northampton players to task after the 1-1 draw with Middlesbrough, describing it as 'a ragged and unconvincing Cobblers performance'. He added: 'The team lacked the bite and polish that saw them through at Maine Road and the hitherto solid defence looked far from steady on several occasions.'

Were these really the players who would shortly launch Northampton into Division One? As if castigating a string of middle-school under-achievers, the reporter's appraisal was severe, from which few were spared. Lines ('a poor match until late in the second half'), Livesey ('energetic but shooting lacked direction'), Hunt ('right out of touch'), Martin ('foraged well but most of his shots long range and didn't hurt'), Everitt ('given the run around by winger Kaye'), Foley ('too often caught out of position') and Leck ('had his hands full ensuring sharpshooter Irvine didn't hammer one home') all came under some sort of fire. Reading all that, it would be easy to assume relegation would be a likelier conclusion to the next eight months' events.

A 0-2 defeat in the blazing sun at Southampton hardly augured well for the re-arranged match with Newcastle, who arrived unbeaten, after taking seven points from their first four games, including 1-0 wins at Charlton and Huddersfield, and a 2-1 home victory over Southampton.

Joe Harvey's Magpies had finished eighth the previous season, in which they failed to beat the Cobblers. Even though they lined up with internationals such as defender Bobby Moncur (Scotland), David Craig (Northern Ireland) and Trevor Hockey (Wales) – as well as Dave Hilley and Ron McGarry – they were destined to find Northampton an awkward stumbling block once more.

The previous March the teams had drawn 2-2, with goals coming from Bobby Hunt on his debut and Derek Leck (Alan Suddick and Bob Cummings scoring for the Magpies). The irony here was that Newcastle's £14,000 bid for Hunt had been turned down by Colchester, and they had instead turned to Scunthorpe's Barrie Thomas.

The Cobblers would have had mixed feelings about the draw, as they had already recorded a 3-2 victory at St James' Park in October 1963. That had initially seemed unlikely when Branston conceded an early penalty which Jim Iley put away. After eighteen minutes striker Kane had gone off with a cut head, staying off the field for fifteen minutes as the Cobblers persevered with ten men. On the stroke of half-time Martin had equalised, only for Colin Taylor to restore the home side's advantage eight minutes after the restart. The fact that Kane levelled with a header after his earlier knock spoke volumes for the bravery of the side. It was Hails, one of two North-East boys in the Cobblers line-up (along with Tommy Robson) who snatched a 68th-minute winner with a cross-cum-shot. With goalkeeper Harvey a former Newcastle player, the victory was especially sweet.

Fast-track events to 8 September almost a year later. Bowen made his first changes of the season, bringing in Billy Best and Brian Etheridge for Martin and Hunt. It was to prove a memorable night for Northampton-born Etheridge, as his late 'rebound' winner at the traditional home Hotel End was to prove his only first-team goal in a claret and white shirt. The victory triggered the seventeen-match unbeaten run which formed the spine of the promotion campaign, a run which ironically was to end at Newcastle on 12 December.

Etheridge had made his Cobblers debut at Notts County nearly two and a half years earlier, in one of the games blessed by a Holton hat-trick, the young hopeful having turned eighteen just a month earlier.

He recalled: 'It was a great day and I enjoyed the game but it was over so quickly.' Subsequent opportunities proved sparse and he would not be the only local lad who needed to move away to truly develop. Etheridge had shown enough promise to be part of an international youth tour of Romania in 1962 – with Don Martin, Graham Carr and Tommy Robson – while also captaining England's amateur youth side on eight occasions, winning twelve caps in all, both as an amateur and professional.

After signing for Brentford in February 1966, Etheridge made 22 league appearances for the Bees before moving to Belgium, where he had two seasons each with Royal Daring FC and FC Bruges. 'I played for Daring in the UEFA Cup and remember matches with the likes of Feyenoord, Strasbourg, Roma and Lausanne … That wouldn't have happened if I'd stayed at Brentford,' said Etheridge.

That 1-0 win over Newcastle was the first of twelve single-goal victories achieved in the league that season. The heavy scoring which distinguished lower division success had already been consigned to the history books. Finding the net with consistency was more of a challenge at the higher level, a situation Hunt and Livesey were unable to rectify to any substantial degree.

The club record 109 league goals scored during the Division Three championship season had been almost halved (58) during the first Division Two season. Now, in winning promotion to Division One, the sparse number of home goals (37) was bettered by fourteen of the other 21 clubs, including both relegated clubs, Swindon and Swansea.

Hunt's £20,000 arrival from Colchester in March of the previous season had been warmly applauded. He came from a footballing family, with his father Ted a strong influence, while Ronnie was the best known of his three playing brothers – a terrier-like midfielder for Colchester who would be killed in a car accident. Hunt's other brothers, Billy and Peter, also skirted the fringes of the full-time game.

Hunt had been a prolific marksman for the Layer Road club, in particular during 1961-62, when Benny Fenton's side had swept to promotion behind Millwall. Even though his official league tally was reduced from 39 to 38 goals when Accrington Stanley folded mid-season – one goal being wiped out – 38 remains a record for Colchester. Hunt's overall record of 99 goals in 164 matches for the 'U's needs no great analysis. In the 9-1 win over Bradford City over Christmas 1961, both he and strike partner Martyn King hit four goals apiece. Bizarrely, City had won the first match 4-1 four days earlier. Hunt, a jaunty individual, had a flair for twists and turns which enabled him to shrug off defenders and deliver incisive crosses and shots. He also fired four goals in a 5-3 win over Doncaster in Colchester's last match of that season.

After scoring three goals for the Cobblers at the back end of 1963-64, Hunt was quickly off the blocks in the victory at Manchester City but the twin gremlins of injuries and travelling – which were to take a toll on his career – were about to rear their ugly heads. Hunt needed cartilage surgery after the goalless draw with Norwich in early November 1964, which meant a five-month break, restricting his 1964-65 appearances to just eighteen in league and cup. He found himself even more sparingly used the following season.

As Hunt told me himself: 'I scored 99 goals for Colchester and ended up only getting around 120 in my career which means I spent the best part of nine years scoring another twenty goals. I never wanted to move away from Colchester when I was a player and it was the travelling which held me back.'

Hunt served six league clubs in all, also playing for Millwall (where he again teamed up with Benny Fenton), Ipswich, Charlton and Reading. The Reading deal came after Hunt had been on loan to Northampton in 1972, when he scored three goals in five matches, only to turn to Elm Park when that club offered a better financial package.

Hunt's finest hour of the Division Two season was his home hat-trick which defeated Ipswich 3-2 on 29 September. That was a night when his combination with Livesey clicked perfectly, as the latter had a hand (or a head) in all three goals. Hunt fired the Cobblers into a 2-0 lead before John Colrain pulled one back. Headers by Etheridge and Livesey teed Hunt up for his third, before Joe Broadfoot – who would sign for the Cobblers in Division One – reduced the deficit once more.

That victory sent Bowen's men joint top of the table, although they were assisted in staying there by Newcastle's 1-2 defeat by Plymouth 24 hours later. The result barely did Ipswich justice, as the visitors struck both posts, through Scottish striker Colrain in the first half, and the bar via Mick McNeil in the second. Although winning, the Cobblers' run of four straight clean sheets came to an end. As for Ipswich, on the day of the match they had lined up Watford's Bill McGarry as their new manager, succeeding Jackie Milburn.

Meanwhile, Livesey was giving supporters a tantalising glimpse of his capabilities, not least during the Friday night visit of Huddersfield. It brought a 3-2 victory against a club which Bowen's men had twice beaten 1-0 the previous season in their first ever league meetings. On this occasion, and with the scores level five minutes before half-time, Livesey struck with a stunning solo effort, capping a strong run from halfway with a 25-yard drive. A Robson double completed the job.

If Livesey didn't provide an avalanche of goals at Northampton, he was at least weighing in with plenty of notable assists. Following a goalless draw at Ipswich on the Tuesday, the Cobblers recorded an acclaimed 1-0 win at Coventry on 19 September, the club's first there since 1955-56 – and before that you had to go back to 1930-31.

Coventry had attracted their biggest post-war league gate during the midweek 0-2 defeat by Derby. Their early season fizz deserted them and they slumped to a fourth straight defeat, Jimmy Hill electing to leave out Hudson from an attack led by George Kirby.

Thousands of Cobblers supporters made the hop to Highfield Road, where with fourteen minutes remaining, goalkeeper Bob Wesson saw his clearance intercepted by Livesey, whose pass allowed Robson to shoot home from thirty yards. Four days later, the Cobblers embarked on a League Cup run which would eventually take them to the quarter-finals, when they won 2-0 at Bournemouth. Walden converted a Robson centre and Livesey's chip over the Cherries' defence allowed Hunt to head the second.

Born in West Ham on 6 February 1938, Livesey had begun his career as an amateur at Wolves but he first came to public awareness when he fired fourteen goals in 25 league games for Southampton during 1958-59, including four against Hull and three against Wrexham.

He then spent two seasons with Chelsea, where he partnered a youthful Jimmy Greaves in Division One, before moving on to Gillingham for a year, then signing for Watford, the club he loved best of all, in October 1962. His cavalier displays almost inspired a first ever season in Division Two for the Hornets. Swept on by Livesey's goals, Watford finished third in Division Three in 1963-64 behind Coventry and Crystal Palace, but of course only two were promoted. In all, he helped himself to 26 goals in 64 league matches for the Vicarage Road club, including a home strike during a 2-1 win over Oldham in February 1964 which has been labelled the greatest in Watford's history.

Livesey's greatest assets were his strength and speed, an ability to shield the ball from opponents, along with an acute eye for goal, which he backed up with a fierce shot. As a character, he had a flair for wheeler-dealing and a 'fun at all costs' approach to life which made him a popular figure in dressing rooms.

Bowen clearly saw Livesey as an answer to his goal-dilemma but the striker spent only just over a year at the County Ground before moving to Brighton, where he ended his professional career by enjoying another three seasons, although he played non-league for Crawley Town. Livesey died from asbestosis at the age of 67 in February 2005.

If Livesey's love-affair was with Watford, Northampton has attracted its own legion of servants who at times have appeared to be fixed magnet-like to the football club, and all that goes with it. Bowen of course, is the classic case. Take out nine years with Arsenal from the time he signed in 1947 to his death in September 1995 and you are left with 39 years of almost limpet-like attachment.

Building teams was his strength though, and there can be no doubting the contributions of such stalwarts as Roly Mills, Jack Jennings and Joe Payne, who all played significant 1960s' roles in the push to the top under his leadership.

Jennings, who began his working life as a railway fireman, was born at Platt Bridge on 27 June 1902. His football career kicked off at Wigan Borough, before he joined Cardiff, where he spent five years from 1925 as a sturdy full-back and wing-half. In 1930, so the story goes, Middlesbrough chairman Phil Bach and manager Peter McWilliam took a train to Ninian Park with the intention of signing Jennings. They ended up prising away three players for £850.

Jennings spent six years at Ayresome Park, during which he was twelfth man for the Football League against the Scottish League at Ibrox. He then spent one season at Preston and another at Bradford City.

His first involvement at Northampton was as a player during the Second World War, and this strict disciplinarian whose sergeant-major training style made players blanch, remained with the club until the end of 1963-64. Jennings also toured the world with the MCC and had a global contacts book until his death in 1977.

The fact that Jennings twice stepped into Bowen's management shoes during periods of illness, and kept the ship stable, reveals the respect in which he was held. That didn't prevent the players removing the odd link in his bicycle chain on more than one occasion, forcing him to push it back to the County Ground after supervising a ten-mile training run.

Next along came Irving Ernest Henry Payne, known affectionately as 'Joe'. A Welshman like Bowen, Payne was born at Briton Ferry in 1921 and had a wartime career as a winger or inside-forward with Swansea, Chester, Wrexham, York and Lovells Athletic, although at the sharp end he also played an active role in the D Day landings.

After the war Payne played for Swansea, Newport and Scunthorpe before signing for the Cobblers in 1951, scoring a hat-trick in nineteen minutes in his second match, a 5-0 victory against Newport. Although he hung up his boots at the end of that season, he began a fifteen-year association as a club trainer, largely with the reserves, until Jennings left the club in 1964, causing his elevation to the first team.

The subtle shift in coaching personnel came at a suitable time for Roly Mills, who had made the last of his 327 league and cup appearances – from his debut at Colchester in 1954, in a 1-2 defeat at Preston – in the final league game of 1963-64. This was Preston's last game before their 2-3 defeat by West Ham in the FA Cup final.

Having embarked as a player with the Cobblers' Town League park side at the age of fourteen, Mills' proud boast was that he played in every outfield position bar centre-half for the Cobblers, beginning as a winger but settling to spend most of his time at wing-half.

He also weighed in with 33 goals during that time, the last of them in a 2-1 win over Portsmouth at the end of March 1964. In that match he galvanised his teammates to help end a run of five matches without victory by firing home from the edge of the penalty area with eighteen minutes left, to add to Foley's first-half penalty. That ensured they survived a late Ron Saunders goal after Everitt had miskicked.

The link with Saunders was in itself fitting, as the vastly experienced centre-forward, who would make his name in management with Norwich and Aston Villa, had been among Mills' teammates – along with Johnny Haynes and Gordon Jago – when he toured France with the England youth party during 1951-52.

Mills' new responsibility was running the reserve team in the Football Combination, at a time when the Cobblers regularly competed against the elite at this level and attracted crowds of 8,000-9,000. While Bowen's most immediate thoughts surrounded Division One survival the following season, Mills' reserves were to finish fourth in a Combination behind Tottenham, Arsenal and Peterborough.

The significance of Bowen's back-up crew became apparent on Saturday, 3 October. When the dust had settled on the afternoon's events, Northampton Town were top (outright) in Division Two, the highest position they had ever reached. The result which took them there was a 2-2 draw at Preston, where they had to withstand a furious second-half onslaught to preserve their precious point. All the more remarkable, granted the fact that Bowen was around 200 miles away at the time.

Bowen's appointment as Welsh team manager was the root cause of his split commitments, and this was his first match in charge. But by the Saturday evening he had cause for double celebration, with the Welsh inflicting a 3-2 defeat on Scotland at Ninian Park in front of 50,000 spectators in the first of that year's Home Internationals. The beautiful twist to the tale is that Ken Leek – the ex-Cobblers striker, now playing for Birmingham – not only grabbed Wales's 87th-minute equaliser, but also pounced for the winner two minutes later.

The fates seem to have conspired to hoist Bowen and the Cobblers to national eminence that day. Journalist Fred Speakman, who for many years covered both football and cricket in Northamptonshire, previewed in a local paper: 'Bowen is with his Welsh team, but Joe Payne knows the policy.'

And so he did, although it helped that, at Deepdale, the hosts were in accommodating mood. Firstly, the match-day programme printed a league table which placed the Cobblers ahead of Newcastle and Norwich. All three had fourteen points but both the Magpies (16-9) and the Canaries (19-12) had a better goal-average than the Cobblers (12-8). It seems the programme editor simply knew something.

The Preston game would have been remarkable without events elsewhere, as it saw three goals in the first eight minutes. Walden fired the visitors ahead in the opening seconds, only for Alex Dawson to equalise. Robson made it 2-1, but Brian Godfrey scored on the half-hour. Of course, a point shouldn't have been enough to send the Cobblers to the top, but results elsewhere smiled on them.

Bowen could have settled for Newcastle's 1-3 defeat at Ipswich, plus a 2-1 win for Charlton over Norwich. However, three other clubs – Rotherham, Bolton and Derby – would all have joined the Cobblers on fifteen points had they won. Instead they all lost. Bolton set the tone for the weekend by going down 1-2 at local rivals Bury on the Friday, while 24 hours later Manchester City defeated Rotherham 2-1 and Swindon came to life with a 4-2 win over Derby.

A healthy cushion would not have been the description, when the Cobblers woke up on Sunday morning to reveal a cluster of clubs breathing down their necks. But they were top, at least for another three days.

CHAPTER FOUR

DEFEND AND BE DAMNED

More than thirty years after making the last of his 444 professional league appearances for three clubs, Terry Branston found himself buying a season ticket at Northampton Town's Sixfields Stadium. This should tell the casual reader at least three things.

Firstly, Branston retains a strong sense of loyalty to the club where he spent the first eight years of his playing career. Secondly, that his appetite for the game, which many players lose shortly after hanging up their boots, has largely survived any middle-aged cynicism or sense of grudge usually brought on by lack of a significant pay-back. Indeed, a day or so after becoming the latest in a long line of ex-pros to have his second knee replacement, Branston settled down to watch Liverpool's 2005 Champions League triumph over AC Milan in Istanbul with all the enthusiasm of a starry-eyed schoolboy. Finally, Branston's 'simply one of the fans' status confirmed a belief held in these parts that Northampton Town, perhaps like many others, has never been a rich club and could perhaps do more to welcome back its 'old boys'.

It might be inappropriate, given the nature of Branston's latter-day injuries, to say that, during Northampton's meteoric rise, mention of his name provoked an automatic 'knee-jerk' reaction (probably a fierce blow to the back of the groin). However, it did. Memories of the team's uncompromising style, egged on by a work-rate which nullified any lack of class in a situation dictated by lack of finance, were instantly conjured up over the years when dropped in polite conversation to the likes of say, Ian St John, Denis Law, Jimmy Greaves or Geoff Hurst. The battering carried out by the likes of Branston, Kurila, Everitt and Foley allowed the playmakers, such as Kiernan, Lines and Leck, to go about their more constructive business.

Branston never moved far from his home town of Rugby, although he joined Luton in 1967 and played a key part in their Division Four championship-winning side under Allan Brown in his first season. Branston spent three years there before ending with Lincoln. The Imps missed promotion by one point in 1971-72, when the Cobblers had to apply for re-election. Then he was pipped for the manager's post by young Graham Taylor in a split 5-4 directors' vote. No great shame in that, although he still harbours the odd regret at not staying in the game. 'I had the chance of coming back as a coach for Dave Bowen in the early 70s,' he said.

Branston's story is like that of a steadily maturing oak. He signed for the Cobblers under Dave Smith as far back as 1958 after being picked up by scout Jack Hastings, but didn't make his first team debut until 1960 at Peterborough, the game where the Cobblers lost a 3-0 lead after Fowler went off injured: 'They didn't take a lot of notice of me to begin with and I was 22 by the time I played in the first team. I had a trial at Notts County but had to ring their manager Tommy Lawton to say I had been made an offer at Northampton. To begin with I was playing for the "A" team at the Symingtons Sports Ground in Market Harborough alongside the likes of Freddie Ramscar – and what a gentleman he was.'

When Branston did earn a regular place, his character brought a light-hearted dressing room influence which helped defuse some of the more intense moments. He recalled a trip to Crystal Palace where his dispute with Chic Brodie over a conceded goal ended with a bag of tomatoes smacked over his head by the goalkeeper. 'I used to bring the lads these tomatoes as they had plenty at the place I was living at the time. It was unusual to have any sort of argument but I ended the day sitting on the coach with tomatoes running down my shirt.'

He also had a more than healthy respect for the man conjuring up the soccer miracle. 'Dave Bowen knew how to get the best out of people. I remember once coming off at half-time thinking I had done quite well as we were winning 1-0, and he tore me right off a strip in the dressing room. Of course I reacted, but when we were running out for the second half, Theo told me not to be so stupid because it was just Bowen's way of keeping me going. He was clever like that. He was good at getting the best out of people and everyone was different and needed handling in different ways.'

Branston's switch to football had meant leaving the British Thompson Houston Company in Rugby which made turbines and where he was a 'jack of all trades' welder. From 1964 he developed his interest in driving, which would eventually see him become an instructor, the career he sustained for 25 years after his playing days ended. 'I taught Barry Lines, Jim Hall and Colin Milburn to drive, among others,' he said. 'I remember Colin being very nervous, which is funny when you think how assured he could be when going out to bat to score 90-odd against the West Indies at Lord's. Dave Bowen used to joke and say I was a part-time footballer and full-time driving instructor!'

Branston's debut at Peterborough was an isolated show, coming as it did when Mills went down with flu, and it took another four months before he popped up again, finally playing the final fifteen games of that season. From that point on, progress was smoother. Terry missed just one league game a season for the next three years. On the last two occasions his deputy was Graham Carr, who would again step in when Branston needed a cartilage operation in March 1964, ruling him out for the last seven games of that campaign.

Every Cobblers player from the early 1960s has a story about the legendary Cliff Holton, and Branston is no exception. He said: 'I remember playing at Coventry, where I was picked up by the team coach at the Dilke Arms at Ryton on Dunsmore, as it was on the way. Cliff wanted to see his relatives in Coventry and said to Dave Bowen: "Branno can take me there – we won't let you down and we'll see you at the ground."

'You wouldn't get away with it these days, but off we went in my Morris Series E. Cliff had the seat right back – it seemed about three or four feet – and was treating me as though I was his chauffeur by saying 'Home James' – and other compliments like that. Of course, we made it to the game in time. Cliff could get away with murder like nobody else but you couldn't see it happening nowadays.'

The other player in the 'special' mould who made a deep impression on those around him was Scottish inside-forward John Reid. He had helped Hamilton Accies to second spot in the Scottish Second Division, joining the Cobblers from Bradford City in November 1961 before switching to Luton for £13,000, thus earning the Cobblers a tidy £8,000 profit. Branston followed an identical path to Kenilworth Road three years later. '[Reid] was a lovely guy and such a good player. While the rest of us had Cortinas for a heart, John Reid had a Rolls Royce.'

Branston further developed his 'dependable rock' influence in the first half of 1964-65, at the hub of a defence which was earning a miserly reputation – Leck's keenness to developing his more attacking wing-half role making his reliability all the more crucial.

The Cobblers had gone top of Division Two at Preston in early October 1964 but they held that position only four days, despite earning a point in an enthralling 3-3 draw at Fratton Park, with Branston scoring one of the only two goals he ever hit in a Cobblers shirt. It was a heroic display, typical of the season in all but the 'goals conceded' column. A campaign noted for defensive solidarity was punctuated by the occasional blip which usually had legitimate excuses – lost 2-4 at Swindon (reshuffle after Branston's injury), 0-5 at Newcastle (Robson's injury early in the game), 2-5 at Plymouth (still celebrating promotion two days earlier and unnerved by a plane journey), and 1-4 at Chelsea in the FA Cup (let's face it, The Pensioners were second in Division One at the time).

At Portsmouth, the Cobblers clawed back from 0-2 down, thanks to goals by Robson and Livesey, and the second half appeared fated against

Bowen's men, with two goals disallowed, while Everitt was forced to limp the final half-hour out on the wing. Pompey restored their lead with four minutes left, but the Cobblers hit back when Branston foraged upfield for a headed equaliser.

It was a vital psychological blow, given the fact that Portsmouth were likely third round League Cup opponents thirteen days later, although at that stage Watford still stood in their way. So, although the leadership was temporarily lost, with Norwich putting paid to Preston 4-2 at Carrow Road that night, spirits remained high.

Three more days and Bowen's men had restored their pole position. The 1-0 victory over Charlton was hardly classic stuff. Roy Matthews hit the bar for the visitors and Harvey denied Mike Kenning from the spot after bringing down Len Glover, the second of six penalties he would save during the season. The winner though, was at least worth the admission fee, Vic Cockcroft's ball down the line sending Robson away for his third goal in as many league matches, ten minutes after the break.

Plymouth's near faultless home record, of which the Cobblers would soon fall foul, came to their aid when Malcolm Allison's side defeated Norwich 1-0. Mike Trebilcock, who topped Argyle's scoring charts with seventeen goals in league and cup – and who would score two goals in an FA Cup final for Everton – was on target as the Canaries were toppled from their lofty perch.

For two blissful months the Cobblers sailed serenely on their way at the top. Without ever destroying the opposition, Bowen's men did enough to lead a competitive section in which the other leading lights seemed to be always dropping points.

A run of London opponents filled the October fixture-book, interrupted only by the visit of Bury on 24 October and Portsmouth, who had renewed rivalry at the County Ground four days earlier for that third round League Cup-tie.

A week after the Charlton win, Bowen switched his strikers at Leyton Orient, with Jim Hall and Don Martin getting the goals in a 2-2 draw with Benny Fenton's side. Nineteen-year-old Hall replaced Etheridge for his first appearance of the season, while Martin deputised for Hunt. After Hall scored his one goal that season, latching onto Livesey's pass before letting fly to beat George Ramage, Martin salvaged a point when he fired home a Robson pass in the second half. In between times, Terry Price had bagged a double, quickly equalising after Branston had blocked a Harry Gregory shot and making it 2-1 shortly after the break.

Norwich though, kept up the pressure with a 3-2 win over Bolton, while Newcastle won 2-1 at Bury. But it was Rotherham who had moved briefly into second spot, on the back of a 4-4 draw at Ipswich and a 4-2 home win over Plymouth.

The momentum was sustained, although in somewhat subdued fashion, on the Tuesday night when Portsmouth were sent tumbling from the League Cup 2-1. Bowen was absent, in Copenhagen for Wales' World Cup qualifier, which they lost 0-1.

Livesey and Martin fired goals into the Spion Kop to reward a decent first-half display. Livesey was unmarked when Martin headed down a Robson corner, while Martin leapt with goalkeeper John Milkins to touch home the second following Barry Cordjohn's wayward back-header. Pompey had needed a replay and extra-time to defeat Watford in the previous round and nearly extended this tie, ultimately having just Tony Barton's second-half goal to show for their efforts.

Bowen kept the same side for the third match running for the visit of Bury, who were beaten 2-0, both goals arriving inside a five-minute spell just after half-time. Newcastle were still breathing down their necks after a 2-0 win over Crystal Palace, even if Rotherham lost 0-2 at Bolton and Norwich suffered the same score at Middlesbrough.

Palace were next up, and despite having made his Arsenal debut fourteen years earlier, master entertainer Holton still had another three years of his career to run. This included a second spell at Watford, before seasons with Charlton and Leyton Orient were fitted in before he hung up his boots in 1967.

How typical that Holton should remind his former teammates of his talents. Indeed, he topped the Palace scoring charts that season with seventeen in league and cup. He netted a cracking late equaliser at Selhurst Park that day, even if his thunder was stolen by Livesey's even later winner, when he headed in a Walden centre. All this came after Robson had broken the deadlock on the hour.

The Holton link, coupled with the fact the two sides' recent history had run along parallel lines, gave Palace fixtures an 'edge' at this time, so the fact that the Palace 'Club Notes' paid tribute to the Cobblers was of added significance. They read: 'Northampton come here today as leaders of the Second Division. No one has beaten them in their last ten Football League and two League Cup games. This week, a national newspaper, in assessing them over their last three matches, described them as "an example to clubs who lack the financial resources and the support to vie with the Tottenhams and Evertons in the transfer market … a triumph for planning and realism".'

The Cobblers had never before reached the fourth round of the League Cup, then in its fifth year, and they were about to take matters a stage further. Fourth Division Chesterfield arrived on the Wednesday evening for the first ever meeting of the clubs. The Saltergate club had by-passed the Cobblers when relegated to Division Four in 1961.

The visitors had bounced to this stage thanks to wins over Hartlepool (3-0), Bristol Rovers (2-0) and Carlisle (3-1), with the much travelled former Norwich, Grimsby and Newport striker Ralph Hunt hitting five goals, including a hat-trick against Carlisle. He would die in a car crash just months later.

The tie turned out to be an ill-tempered affair which the Cobblers won 4-1, a margin exaggerated by Martin's second goal of the night and a Foley penalty in the final five minutes, after Walden had been brought down by Albert Holmes.

The Cobblers played the final fifty minutes with ten men following the dismissal of Everitt for kicking Scotsman George Duncan. At this point they were already leading 2-0, after Hunt scored one goal and made another for Martin, before Leck's foul on Mike Commons allowed Gerry Clarke to pull one back from the spot. A quarter-final trip to Plymouth three weeks later beckoned after The Pilgrims had added Stoke City to their list of First Division scalps, after a replay, having already accounted for Sheffield United.

On 7 November it was the turn of Norwich to visit the County Ground. The Canaries had dropped to fifth but were only four points adrift of Bowen's men and had shown their pedigree the week before by holding Newcastle 1-1 at Carrow Road, a result which ensured Newcastle were just two points in arrears of Bowen's men.

Northampton was buzzing. While the first team had been winning at Palace seven days earlier, a Billy Best hat-trick and a goal from Barry Lines had helped condemn Arsenal's reserves to a 4-0 defeat in the Football Combination.

The Norwich game, though, proved an anticlimax. The Canaries had drawn for the first time in the league seven days earlier, and now added a goalless stalemate. Newcastle's 3-1 win over Rotherham reduced the gap at the top to a single point. Palace's recovery from their Cobblers defeat with a 1-0 win at Southampton, and Bolton's 3-1 success at the expense of Derby ensured the sides which had begun the day in third and fourth places lost valuable momentum.

It was Branston who again earned the plaudits a week later as Leck's first goal of the season earned a point in a 1-1 draw at Rotherham, who put the brake on three straight defeats. Danny Williams' side had completed a double over Bowen's men the previous season, including a 3-1 victory at the County Ground on Boxing Day.

Lines came in for the injured Hunt, and somehow the Cobblers held the lead given them when Leck fired past Roy Ironside in the seventeenth minute until midway through the second half, when Ian Butler levelled. With Newcastle losing 1-3 at Swansea, it meant a two-point cushion for Northampton once more before the visit of the Swans the following Saturday.

The 2-1 score in that match might not sound convincing, but the Cobblers produced a performance of promotion standard, with Walden's return after a one-match absence proving the inspiration. Walden's flair for attacking defenders on the Cobblers' right flank had to be harnessed with some thought for cover, a task to which this product of the small Northants village of Walgrave, off the Kettering Road, showed rather less enthusiasm.

Walden recalled the Division Two philosophy and regular team-talk which rammed down the words: 'We've got a point for a start. Let's hang onto it, and see if we can pinch two.' Years later he was still haunted by three different voices. Two thirds of the nightmare was the combined force of Bowen and Foley screeching: 'Harry, get back!'. The other came from an old Northampton fan, whose name he never knew, but who he could guarantee bumping into at least once a year in the town's busy centre to remind him of the day he nearly sank the 1965-66 league champions when through on goal against Tommy Lawrence. This character would always stop him and say: 'Harry, remember Liverpool … you should have scored that day but ended up taking the ball out by the left corner flag.'

The eleven league goals which Walden netted for Luton proved a better return than the three he fired for the Cobblers in 76 matches. One of his other career stories revolved around the fact that one week during 1960-61 he was playing in Kettering's reserves, and the next he was in Luton's first team in Division Two.

Walden was always stronger on 'assists', and against Swansea he opened up the visitors early on, beating two men before firing a shot which goalkeeper Noel Dwyer could only parry, allowing Robson to nip in to drill home the loose ball. The Swans equalised when George Kirby headed past Harvey, but the Cobblers regained the lead midway through the second period when Martin hacked the ball home, following a pass from Lines. At the death, it was Everitt who saved the day, clearing off the line when left-half Bert Williams' shot had Harvey beaten.

The League Cup bubble though, was about to pop, with a string of injury problems contributing to the downfall at Home Park on the Wednesday evening. Argyle, with Malcolm Allison in his first spell as manager, were on a high. They were about to stretch their unbeaten home run to twenty games and had moved into third place in the Division Two table on the previous Saturday with a 3-2 victory over Manchester City, who Allison would join the following July as assistant to Joe Mercer.

The task for Bowen's men was made harder when Duncan Neale broke the offside trap in the eighth minute, allowing John Newman to score what turned out to be the winner.

Absent from the Cobblers ranks through injury were Leck, Everitt, Martin and Robson, and while Bobby Brown (making his first appearance of the season), Kurila, Hall and Cockcroft came in, they couldn't prevent the Pilgrims' march to a two-legged semi-final date with Leicester where, after losing the first leg 2-3, they were defeated 0-1 at home in front of 20,780, some 1,188 fewer than watched the Northampton tie. After the Cobblers fell behind, Brown, Kurila and Livesey were all denied by goal-keeper Dave Maclaren. Plymouth also included Tony Book, who would later follow Allison to Maine Road.

All bar Everitt returned for the league game at Derby on the Saturday, where goals by Brown and Martin earned a point in a 2-2 draw. Cobblers' relief that Rams' top scorer Eddie Thomas was ruled out through injury proved short-lived. Robson was in the wars and was forced off with a gashed forehead after a clash with Derby's Geoff Barrowcliffe. It was while the Cobblers were down to ten men that they fell behind. They twice fought back, firstly when Martin outpaced the Derby defence to fire home from twenty yards; then with the Cobblers trailing 1-2, late in the game, Brown headed in a Walden cross for the equaliser.

Brown had been signed the previous December from Watford, where he had turned professional after playing as an amateur with Barnet and Fulham. Being an amateur allowed him to represent Great Britain in the 1960 Rome Olympics, where he played in a victory over China as well as a 2-2 draw with Italy and a 3-4 defeat by Brazil.

In all, Brown won fourteen England amateur caps and another ten for Great Britain. His other notable achievement as an amateur was scoring twice at Wembley for Barnet in their 2-3 defeat by Crook Town in the 1958-59 Amateur Cup final. In 1961 he was a member of the FA tour to the Far East, New Zealand and San Francisco, a party which also included Laurie Brown.

It is not surprising that, given his wealth of London contacts, Bowen was aware of, and keen to recruit Brown. However, his perseverance was tested, as Brown recalled: 'When I was at Barnet I used to train midweek evenings, after which it was 23 stops home on the Tube. On at least four or five occasions while I was there a car would pull up alongside me as I walked to the station and the man inside offered to give me a lift. It was Dave Bowen.'

It is a testament to Brown that although he didn't make his first appearance of 1964-65 until late November, he should end up as joint top league scorer with thirteen, although Martin's three League Cup goals gave him an overall edge.

Signed as a makeweight when Bryn Jones went to Watford to be re-united with manager Ron McGarry, Brown found himself once more in the company of Livesey, to whom he had played second fiddle at Vicarage Road. Although he didn't instantly figure as a first-team regular, Brown played alongside his fellow Londoner for the second half of 1964-65 and made a deeper impression in Division One.

Brown was back on the scoresheet the following weekend when Swindon were beaten 2-1 at the County Ground, with Robson firing the other. Swindon had been promoted with the Cobblers two seasons earlier and, bristling with the talents of Mike Summerbee, John Trollope and Don Rogers, forged ahead when Dennis Brown hacked a shot past Harvey. The Cobblers levelled when Tony Hicks dropped a centre at Robson's feet, before Brown crashed home a left-foot drive from thirty yards. That made it seventeen league games without defeat for the Cobblers, but this epic run was about to end, with the trip to St James' Park just seven days away.

Newcastle went into the contest just two points behind Bowen's men, having won 6-1 at Swindon and 3-0 over Portsmouth, a game in which Trevor Hockey had scored his first goal in a Magpies shirt since joining from Nottingham Forest. Newcastle were well aware that victory of any sort would bring them back the leadership on goal-average and a crowd of 40,376, their biggest gate of the season, were there to see whether Joe Harvey's men could pull it off.

Cup distractions were no problem for Newcastle. They bowed out of both competitions at the first hurdle without scoring a goal, losing 0-3 at Division One Blackpool in the League Cup, and allowing Swansea brief respite from their relegation struggles by going down 0-1 at the Vetch Field in January.

Spice to the Newcastle clash was added by the fact the Cobblers had done their best the previous season to try to prevent rivals Sunderland from being promoted to Division One behind champions Leeds, completing a league double over them. Bowen had then been offered the management post at Roker Park as a successor to Alan Brown, but turned it down.

In addition to Cobblers with past North-East connections – such as Robson, Harvey and Kiernan – Newcastle had Welsh internationals Ollie Burton and Dave Hollins, players who were only too acutely aware of Bowen's depth of tactical know-how. Here though, the Cobblers were to be badly out of luck, although their 0-5 hammering had a bizarre tale attached to it.

Although Hockey's second goal in a Newcastle shirt had quickly put the home side on course, the Cobblers were handicapped when Robson left the field after seventeen minutes with concussion. He also suffered three teeth knocked out and a broken jaw. Yet four minutes before the interval it was still 0-1, with the ten-man Cobblers somehow holding their own.

At this point (or so the story goes) manager Bowen went down to the dressing room to check up on Robson. In his absence there ensued a calamitous four minutes which saw Newcastle's Bill McGarry (who topped their scoring charts that season with sixteen) hit the target twice inside two minutes, while an Everitt own-goal compounded the Cobblers' misery.

The roars would have been considerable, but locked away in the Cobblers' dressing room, much of this was lost on Bowen as he surveyed his wounded and dizzy star. When the players descended a few minutes later, the pep talk began on the premise that the score was still 0-1 before a voice piped up: 'No hang on a minute, boss, it's not 1-0 any longer, it's now 4-0 to Newcastle ...' A marked silence followed before the reply (insert your own Welsh accent) 'Sorry?' 'We're 4-0 down?' 'Oh well, that puts a slightly different light on it. Roll up your sleeves, I think it's time for damage limitation now lads!'

In the circumstances, the Cobblers came out of the afternoon quite well. The ten men held on grimly until McGarry completed his hat-trick with a minute to go, after which most thoughts turned to the visit of Manchester City the following Saturday, the last game before Christmas.

Although Newcastle went to the head of the table in style, the Cobblers still held a three-point gap over third-placed Norwich, who led Bolton on goal-difference. Bolton appeared on the festive Christmas menu twice, so there was little reason to be downbeat for long.

CHAPTER FIVE

COBBLERS ARE THERE!

Beautiful in its simplicity, awesome in dramatic effect. This was the headline which screamed out from the front page of Northampton's *Green 'Un* on the Saturday evening of 17 April 1965. Tiny head shots of sixteen Cobblers players who had helped gain promotion, were lined up across the top of the page. Underneath read the score: Bury 1 Northampton Town 4, along with the words: 'Now Booked For First Division …'

It's still hard to comprehend how it happened but the facts are there, staring boldly from the football record books. Of the final twenty league matches, after the engine fault at Newcastle, nine matches were won, eight were drawn, but crucially only three were lost. While the Cobblers were beaten in only six league matches all season, even Newcastle came off second best on nine occasions.

Loyalty and stickability, a determination not to lose at any cost, had claimed its due reward. How else do you explain the fact that on the day of the Bury game, John Linnell scored twice for the reserves in a 2-2 draw with West Ham? Linnell, a rugged wing-half, was an enduring and endearing character who spent eight years at the County Ground without bursting onto the main stage. He signed professional in 1963 and waited four years for one League Cup show against Rotherham before moving to Peterborough for a season, where he made 26 appearances.

Local, it seemed, was always best. When it came to the chance of signing for Plymouth in 1968-69, Linnell preferred to switch into non-league with Banbury, following his old County Ground inspiration Jack Jennings who was manager at the time. It also allowed him to dedicate more time to his father Vic's business … grave-digger. When I spoke to him many years later, note-book and pen in hand while he dutifully laid out a plot in the Saxon village churchyard in Brixworth, Linnell told me: 'The Cobblers was just a great place with a terrific atmosphere at the time and I didn't want to leave. My father took on this business when he came out of the Army in 1946 and now I have run my own business for 28 years.' No wonder a national newspaper once referred to the Cobblers' ascent as: 'The Rise Of Tombstone Town'.

There were others in the background, loyal and dependable, just waiting for a chance. Full-back Colin Sharpe, who made England youth appearances, keen aspirants such as Roger Barron, Kenny Harrold, John Bates, Gary Fagan, Gary Knibbs, Alan Inwood, Nicky Bamforth, Ray

Price and Ray Perryman. These men formed an expeditionary force, a veritable back-up crew, a vital part of the framework while destined to never climb the most challenging peak.

To an extent, Linnell, Martin, Walden and occasionally Hall – looking up his old mates on a trip back from Caistor – kept up those traditions by gathering for a pint, a game of whist or bingo in the Moulton WMC on a Sunday lunchtime nearly forty years later. Perhaps my imagination is deserting me, but it's hard to see David Beckham, Gary Neville, and Roy Kean enacting the same scenario.

Bowen stepped out of the visitors' dressing room at Gigg Lane on that fateful Saturday and within minutes was on national radio, interviewed by Brian Moore. Despite the Cobblers' victory, the players needed to know Bolton hadn't won at Rotherham to ensure they were definitely up into Division One. Bolton were playing for the second time in 24 hours and, after losing 0-2 at Newcastle on Good Friday, could only draw 0-0 at Millmoor. Bowen told his players as much. 'I just nipped into the dressing room and there was such an outcry I thought the best thing to do was come out,' Bowen told Moore. 'We did take some champagne just in case we won promotion. It seems it was money well spent.'

Bowen (perhaps wisely) refused to be pinned down on how the Cobblers would fare in Division One, preferring to savour the moment, but told Moore: 'When we came out of the Fourth Division, people said we would probably struggle in the Third and when we came out of the Third they said we would probably struggle in the Second.'

He attributed the success to the commitment of the players, saying: 'Nothing is impossible in football with the right kind of people around you if they are prepared to dedicate themselves. It is all down to the boys.' What price loyalty?

'Strolling' Joe Kiernan inspired the victory at Bury that afternoon. He might have left it late to register his first goal of the season that afternoon (he then scored in the next match at Plymouth), but Kiernan's creative genius soon became a focal point for the national scribes keen to pinpoint a reason for the Cobblers' dramatic rise. It seemed only a matter of time before he moved to a more fashionable club, such was his expertise in the role of cultured playmaker. Everton and Arsenal were among those who would try to make that happen with bids of around £40,000. Amazingly, it never did, as Bowen clung onto his star in the way a bird of prey pins its victim.

Kiernan was the nephew of the former Celtic star Tommy Kiernan and was born in Coatbridge. Growing up in Scotland, Kiernan played schools football in the company of Billy Best, but was given his chance by Sunderland, from where he was signed by the Cobblers in 1963. His only league game for the Wearside club was a 4-2 win at Southampton, in which Brian Clough registered a hat-trick. He made his home debut in a 7-1 League Cup victory over Oldham.

Frustrated by his lack of opportunities at Roker, he was still weighing up the chance to join Plymouth, but was swayed by the fierce camaraderie at Northampton. 'There were a couple of ex-Sunderland players at Plymouth and I was going to talk to them. I stopped off at the County Ground and didn't fancy it that much. After all, it wasn't exactly Roker Park. They suggested I watch a friendly at Luton and I saw the likes of Foley, Everitt, Branston, Kurila and Large putting it in and I thought to myself "These players will hold their own in Division Two".'

Kiernan was staying at the Black Lion on Northampton's Marefair, with others from the North East, such as Best and Robson, in the company of landlady Mrs Horn, and was quickly stunned by the side's togetherness: 'I walked into the Dolphin Bar of the Grand Hotel on Gold Street that night and saw fifteen players standing there. I couldn't believe it as nothing like that had happened at Sunderland. I told Theo I was considering going down to Plymouth and he told me "you don't want to go down there" as he had been at Exeter! That just about did it.'

The friendship forged that night has lasted a lifetime, and proved sufficiently powerful for Foley to bring Kiernan in as his assistant when he became the Northampton manager in 1990.

After a stuttering 1963-64 in which he played nineteen league games, Kiernan missed only one the next season, and was to prove an ever-present in Division One. Skipper Foley, goalkeeper Harvey, and Leck were the men with a complete 1964-65 league record, although Leck missed the League Cup defeat at Plymouth through injury.

At Bury, Martin's late run of goals continued with a double. He was to fire six in five games to take his league tally up to thirteen, alongside Brown who also hit the target in the Bury mud. Paul Durrant's first-half goal for the Shakers counted for nothing.

Newcastle's Good Friday win against Bolton had been followed by a 1-1 draw at Crystal Palace and another in the Monday return at Bolton. Newcastle remained in the driving seat, especially when the Cobblers were hammered 2-5 at Plymouth.

Although Newcastle drew 0-0 with Manchester City on the last day of the season, that put the title out of reach for the Cobblers, who played Portsmouth in the evening. Due to the Magpies' better goal-average, the Cobblers would have needed to win 24-0 to overhaul them. In fact, they drew, finishing one point behind, but six clear of third-placed Bolton.

That was how it panned out, but turning the clock back to Christmas, Manchester City, Bolton and Southampton had made a high-profile festive programme, as Bowen's men set out to repair damage inflicted by the Newcastle drubbing.

The City match had brought a repeat score of the sides' early season meeting. There were eleven minutes left when Leck fired the Cobblers ahead from twelve yards but four minutes later it was 2-0. Everitt, having a brief spell at inside-forward, blasted home a 25-yard drive on the turn after a pass by Lines.

That match marked the return of Ken Leek, one of the 1958 heroes of the FA Cup win over Arsenal. Bowen had paid Birmingham £10,000 for his fellow countryman, double what the Cobblers had received from Leicester six years earlier, but only a third of what Birmingham had paid to Newcastle for the same player.

Leek was also in the side which drew 0-0 at Bolton on Boxing Day, an occasion which lived up its streetwise name. Cobblers chairman Fred York labelled 'a disgrace' hooliganism which caused £100 of damage to the team coach. On the field, Bolton goalkeeper Eddie Hopkinson made great saves from Walden and Robson. The draw ended Bolton's run of nine straight home wins, which had lifted them to fourth. The Cobblers became only the third club to prevent Bill Ridding's side from scoring that season, after Swansea and Coventry.

The Bolton return two days later was called off when referee Norman Burtenshaw deemed the pitch unplayable, but it had recovered sufficiently for Southampton to provide the first opposition of 1965. The stage was set for one of goalkeeper Harvey's finest hours.

While luck will always play a part in the giving and taking of penalties, the Cobblers tended to over-ride this issue at this point in their history. Basically, if they were awarded a spot-kick, Foley would tuck it away, and if unlucky enough to give one away, Harvey would save it.

The last time the Cobblers had missed a penalty was during a 2-2 draw with Bournemouth in 1962, when Holton had proved the unlikeliest of culprits. Northampton then converted their next twenty, until Tommy Knox missed one at Reading in August 1968. In between, Everitt, Foley, Reid and John Mackin all contributed to the successful tally, with Foley and Mackin putting away nine apiece.

Saving penalties didn't carry the same guarantee (two flew past Harvey at Plymouth, and Fourth Division Chesterfield had scored one in the League Cup), but Harvey did keep out six during 1964-65 and deservedly dined out on this fact for many years: 'I started to watch people who were taking penalties as they were placing the ball. Few people can resist looking at the spot where they are going to put it. Ninety per cent of the time I guessed right. Mind you it is more difficult these days with softer balls rather than the leather variety we had in those days. In the end only miskicks were going to beat me.'

Harvey used to practise his penalty technique with Foley on the training ground and claimed the Cobblers skipper used to get depressed at his high success rate. Luckily, Foley was rarely daunted when it came to the serious match-day challenge.

Harvey started (or rather stopped) the ball rolling at Ipswich in September by denying Frank Brogan, and then Charlton's Mike Kenning in October. The Southampton game was special though, with two saves from England international Terry Paine, who had beaten him with two during Saints' 3-1 win at The Dell the previous season – a game played the day after President Kennedy's assassination. Harvey extended his sequence by sticking out a foot to divert Francis Lee's effort over the bar against Bolton in March, and also saved from Norwich City's Joe Mullett later that month in a 1-1 draw.

The Southampton match ended 2-2 and was voted by many as one of the most entertaining spectacles in memory. The Saints boasted the division's leading scorer in Gerry O'Brien, who hit three hat-tricks in total, including all four in the 4-0 win over Charlton, while Martin Chivers joined him with a treble in the 6-1 win over Rotherham.

But though future Spurs and England international Chivers scored on this occasion, O'Brien drew a blank. Harvey's second penalty save might have been tempered by Foley heading the resultant corner into his own net, but Branston went upfield to equalise.

Chelsea (away) the following Saturday proved a challenge too far, but at least a quick FA Cup exit allowed Bowen's men to concentrate on more serious matters. It gave a chance for Livesey to impress against his old club and Robson made an impression on Chelsea boss Tommy Docherty, who would sign him by the end of the year.

One report of the game related: 'Northampton often had ten men in their penalty area to stem eager Chelsea attacks.' The Cobblers held out for 44 minutes until a four-man move involving John Hollins, Terry Venables, Barry Bridges and Bobby Tambling ended with Tambling beating Harvey from close range.

Northampton might have equalised when Livesey intercepted a poor back-pass by ex-Cobbler Frank Upton, only for Peter Bonetti to produce one of his famous 'cat'-like reflexes to save. The walls caved in after the break, Bridges making it 2-0 after Tambling had robbed Leck, before a George Graham shot from Tambling's cross was deflected in by Foley.

The Cobblers skipper reduced the arrears from the spot after Hollins pulled down Everitt, only for Bridges to add the fourth.

A 0-2 defeat at Huddersfield, where one of the scorers was Leicestershire county cricketer Chris Balderstone, and a 1-1 draw with local rivals Coventry, hardly captured headlines for the Cobblers for the remainder of January, a month which ended with the side idle, as a result of their FA Cup exit.

Those teams in action on 30 January 1965 wore black armbands in memory of the death of Sir Winston Churchill. Two of the Cobblers' closest rivals, Norwich and Derby, closed the gap after beating Swindon and Manchester City respectively. The Canaries were now within a point of Northampton, who at this stage were a respectful five points adrift of leaders Newcastle.

Perhaps worse for Cobblers fans was Peterborough causing the day's major FA Cup shock, beating Arsenal 2-1 with goals by Derek Dougan and Peter McNamee, after John Radford had given the Gunners the lead before half-time. Posh later went out 1-6 at Chelsea.

The Cobblers returned to action at Ninian Park on 6 February, where Cardiff officials were understandably left querying how their crowd could drop from 50,000 to less than 8,000 in the space of just a few days. It seems Real Zaragoza in midweek qualified as a far bigger draw than did Northampton.

The Bluebirds' European Cup-Winners' Cup quarter-final hangover (they lost 0-1 to exit 2-3 on aggregate) proved just the tonic for Bowen's men, who captured a first win in six matches. A feature of the match was Branston's duel with John Charles, while in the first half the Cobblers' goal led a charmed life. Even though Bob Wilson didn't have a shot to save, Brown missed a glorious chance when through on goal just before the break, only to fire wide of the target.

Brown only played after passing a fitness test on a knee but, ultimately, his contribution proved vital, opening the scoring just after the break following a peach of a pass by Robson. After Brown had added a second, the Cobblers survived another big scare. Harvey denied Derek Tapscott, Bowen's old Arsenal team-mate, the Cobblers goalkeeper turning his shot onto the foot of a post.

Home wins over Preston (2-1) and Leyton Orient (2-0), with a 1-1 draw at Charlton tucked in between, saw the Cobblers return to the top of Division Two, helped by Newcastle's 1-2 loss at Orient and 2-3 defeat at home to Bury.

So when Bolton arrived at the County Ground for the re-arranged Christmas fixture on a Tuesday night in early March, Bowen's men had the chance of extending their lead at the top to three points. How they seized the opportunity.

After reserves and apprentices raked snow from the pitch to ensure the game went ahead, Walden's fourth-minute cross was headed in by Martin. Foley's forty-yard free-kick then confused everybody. Martin and Brown jumped for the ball, along with Bolton's Bryan Edwards, who unsighted Eddie Hopkinson in the Wanderers goal. Harvey needed to be alert when tipping a Brian Bromley overhead kick over the bar, but the Cobblers made it 3-0 when Leck sent Robson scampering free down the left. When the resultant cross was headed clear, Leck half-volleyed back from 25 yards. It only remained for Harvey to keep out Lee's penalty after Leek had handled, and for Brown to centre for Martin to head the fourth, to complete a perfect night for the home side.

However, consecutive 1-1 draws with Crystal Palace and Norwich again left the Cobblers trailing Newcastle on goal-average. The Carrow Road clash was the more memorable, although certainly not for the right reasons. Robson's 25th-minute opener, after Walden and Leck had worked a neat short-corner move, put the Cobblers in the driving seat, but Terry Allcock equalised with a glancing header after a move involving Tommy Bryceland and Don Heath. The Cobblers' offside trap riled the crowd and temperatures rose shortly after half-time. Harvey was booked for a foul on Ron Davies, only to redeem himself by saving the Mullett penalty which resulted, diving on the rebound to complete the save. Branston was injured in the follow-up scuffle, necessitating the cartilage operation which ended his season.

While Brown might have earned both points on the hour, only to fire over after rounding Keelan, the game's other drama was reserved for the final minutes. Robson, forever a jack-in-the-box and irksome to defenders, danced up and down in front of Keelan as the Norwich goalkeeper prepared to boot the ball downfield. Somewhere, something snapped. Keelan punched Robson, removing him of his front teeth in the process. Off went Keelan, adding to the four names already in referee Stokes' note-book (Harvey, Leck and Branston of the Cobblers and City's Phil Kelly being the others).

In the week prior to the game at Swindon, Branston recalled being visited in hospital by a delegation which included Vic Cockcroft, Colin Milburn, Ronnie Walton and Carr: He said: 'Graham was dying for a game in the first team and if I ever got injured he would come into the dressing room to see how I was. On this occasion I remember him looking at my knee and plaster and saying "You won't be playing on Saturday then Terry?"'

The Swindon match programme reminded fans of great rivalries past, including a time when the Cobblers presented the railway town club with a model train with club names inscribed on the carriages in league table order, in recognition of Swindon's success. If anything, the rivalry was now as great as ever.

The Cobblers' other significant team-change saw Hall brought in for Lee, but it was strike partner Brown whose two first-half goals seemed to have decided the destiny of the points, only for Swindon to ease their relegation plight by scoring four – Ernie Hunt (2), Mike Summerbee and Don Rogers were the men on target.

It was a black armband day for the Cobblers in more senses than one. Chairman Fred York had died on the Wednesday, less than a month before his dream of Division One football would be realised. Ted Buller took over the 'acting role'.

Any questions raised over young Carr's ability to step into Branston's shoes were answered by his performances in a 1-0 win over Rotherham, a 2-1 win at Swansea, and a 2-2 draw at home to Derby, just seven days before the crunch match at Bury. Carr had been forced to bide his time, playing just one first-team match in each of the previous two seasons, although there were others who had to be more patient still.

The Swansea win, in particular, suggested the Cobblers were on the verge of something special. Nine visits to the Vetch Field going back to 1919 had brought four draws and five defeats, yet with the impetus of Martin's 25-yard shot which went in off a post in the first five minutes, that dismal record changed, Brown getting the other.

The four goals shared with Derby merely served to tee up the events of a heady Easter, the Bury success followed by two matches with Plymouth. Thankfully the 2-5 crash at Home Park related to events on the field and not to a Cobblers team flying to a match for the first time – from Luton to Exeter Airport. Plymouth were beaten 3-1 in the return the next day, and only Portsmouth remained.

It was a balmy Saturday evening, late in April 1965. In the heart of the Midlands, the shoe industry was hanging on by a thread. Portsmouth were doing something similar with their Division Two status. Events during the afternoon had given the Pompey boys a glimmer of hope on this final day. They might still stay up. After all, wasn't Northampton the place to go for miracles?

The Cobblers had not been beaten at home all season and had already booked their place among the elite for 1965-66. Wolverhampton and Birmingham were coming down and Newcastle and Northampton would be replacing them.

Moore the merrier ... Welsh international Graham Moore included Chelsea, Manchester United and the Cobblers among his six league clubs, and in recent years has run a pub in North Yorkshire

Goodnight in Vienna. Bryan Harvey returns the ball to the centre circle after the Cobblers concede a goal in their 2-2 draw with Rapid Vienna in August 1965

Take-off for Division One. The Cobblers arrive at Exeter Airport prior to their match
with Plymouth in April 1965, two days after clinching promotion at Bury.
From left: Harry Walden, Tommy Robson, Don Martin, Bobby Brown, Bobby Hunt,
Dave Bowen, Joe Kiernan, Graham Carr, Jim Hall, Derek Leck, Joe Payne,
and Mike Everitt. Kneeling, Theo Foley

Inspirational skipper Theo Foley leads the
Cobblers out in Division One in the quest
for more points

Bryan Harvey has Theo Foley in attendance as he pushes the ball away from Keith Todd during the 2-1 win at Swansea Town in April 1965

Cobblers trainer Joe Payne supervises
a training session at the
Old Northamptonians Sports Ground

George Hudson (standing), Vic Cockcroft, John Kurila, Mike Everitt and Joe Kiernan
are among those brushing up on sun-tans during the tour to Germany in May 1966

Fond farewell ... Author Mark Beesley and Dave Bowen bid a nostalgic goodbye to the
Hotel End terraces prior to the club's move to Sixfields in 1994

The men on board. This 1960 shot of Northampton Town directors commemorated the opening of the club's floodlights. Back (from left): Bob Brett, Eric Northover, Archie Whatton. Front: Reggie Saunders, Con Wilson, Wally Penn, Fred York, Ted Buller. Insets: Ken Dear, Dr Hollingsworth

The legendary Cliff Holton, who died in 1995, seen here during his Arsenal days

Terry Branston weaves his way through another training session

Bobby Brown and Don Martin are the Cobblers players in this aerial challenge with
Coventry's George Curtis and Dietmar Bruck during the 1-1 draw at
the County Ground in January 1965

Team tactics. Boss Dave Bowen gives a talk to Terry Branston, Theo Foley, Barry Lines,
Charlie Livesey, Derek Leck and Mike Everitt, while trainer Joe Payne looks on

England amateur international Bobby Brown was the Cobblers' top scorer in Division One and later emulated Dave Bowen by playing a management role for the Welsh national team

Jimmy Greaves appeals for a penalty (and gets it) during the Cobblers' 1-1 draw at Tottenham in April 1966. Notice the Cobblers have two No 10s on the field, substitute Jim Hall and Don Martin

Goalkeeper Norman Coe is in mid-air as Theo Foley and Vic Cockcroft collide.
Rodney March looks on during the 4-1 win at Fulham in November 1965

Winger Joe Broadfoot was bought for
£27,000 midway through the Division
One campaign, but didn't fit comfortably
into the team structure

The problems of sharing a ground with a cricket club are apparent in this *Daily Mail* picture, later presented to the club. It was taken as the club prepared for Division One

September 1967. A Parachute Regiment Royal Horse Artillery helicopter hovers above the County Ground, minutes before the start of a 2-1 home defeat by Reading

Roly Mills (left) served the club in a huge variety of roles during five decades, while trainer
Joe Payne proved a reliable sounding board for Dave Bowen during life at the top

Don Martin had his jaw broken during the
run up to the Division One campaign but still
scored seven goals. He returned in 1975 after
eight years with Blackburn Rovers

Men between the sticks. John Mackin (left) quickly switched from being a goalkeeper to an outfield player, but Chic Brodie (centre) and Norman Coe both wore the No 1 jersey during the climb to Division One

Bryan Harvey is watched by Theo Foley as he makes a save during the 2-0 win at Cardiff City in February 1965

Winger Barry Lines became the first ever player to score for the same club in all four English divisions when he hit the target against West Bromwich Albion at the County Ground in September 1965

Harsh on Marsh … Rodney Marsh is beaten after taking over from the injured Tony Macedo during the Cobblers' 4-1 victory at Craven Cottage in November 1965

It is August 1965 and young supporters, suitably attired, admire the club's coat of arms which is about to be raised for the visit of Manchester United

Jim Hall was an example of 'local boy made good' when he played for the Cobblers in Division One. Supporters warmly remember his thumping header which earned a point at Highbury, and his two goals inside 90 seconds which defeated Aston Villa at the County Ground

The Cobblers' old main stand at the County Ground held the club back and was finally
pulled down in the wake of the Bradford City fire in 1985

Seaside special … Off to Bournemouth in 1963 are (from left) Theo Foley,
Graham Carr, Alec Ashworth, John Kurila, Arnold Woollard and Mike Everitt

Poleaxed … Goalkeeper Norman Coe is surrounded by anxious teammates after being knocked out in the first minute at Stoke City in February 1966

Joker's wild … Graham Carr always brought a strong sense of colour to proceedings, both in the 1960s as a player and then as a Northampton manager twenty years later

Derek Leck became the first of
the class of 1965-66 to wear a
Northampton shirt when he
made his debut at Exeter City
in February 1959

Mike Everitt has just handled a shot on the line at Tottenham in April 1966,
allowing Spurs the chance to draw level from the penalty spot

Joe Kiernan not only played like the legendary Jim Baxter of Sunderland during 1965-66, but he began to look like him as well

Ball games ... Track-suited Cobblers players work out at the Old Northamptonians Sports Ground during the mid-1960s

Catholic boys together … the lengthy friendship enjoyed by Theo Foley and Joe
Kiernan brought them back together again as a managerial team at Northampton in
1990, some 25 years after the club climbed into Division One

Snowbound. Joe Payne, Billy Best, Graham Carr, Vic Cockcroft and John Kurila
inspect an icy County Ground in December 1962

1966 and all that ... a rare Cobblers training team picture which includes Graham
Moore (centre of back row) and George Hudson (second left on front row)

Club historian Frank Grande orchestrated a 1991 players' reunion at the Exeter Rooms
in Northampton, when the author was able meet up with club 'legend' Frank Large

The scene on the cricket side of the County Ground on 23 April, 1966 when 24,523 people squeezed into the County Ground for the crunch game with Fulham

Graham Carr signed from his native North East in 1962 and played 27 times in Division One

Mike Everitt was signed as a right-winger but played most of his Cobblers matches at left-back, which made him incredibly versatile

The County Ground had its drawbacks, but it was always within easy hailing distance of scenic training areas, such as the Old Northamptonians Sports Ground, Abington Park, and the Old Northampton Racecourse

Hurdles to surmount. Theo Foley at work on the Old Northamptonians Sports Ground

Supporters special … Nine trains from Northampton and Wellingborough helped ferry as many as 6,000 fans to Liverpool for the fourth round FA Cup-tie defeat in 1958

Team spirit ... John Reid, Joe Kiernan, Graham Carr, Frank Large, Vic Cockcroft and
Charlie Brodie enjoy a night out ,with a kneeling Tommy Robson

Slipping and sliding ... It is March 1967 and the Cobblers are rapidly falling from grace.
In this match they are beaten 0-2 at Bristol Rovers at the now defunct Eastville Stadium

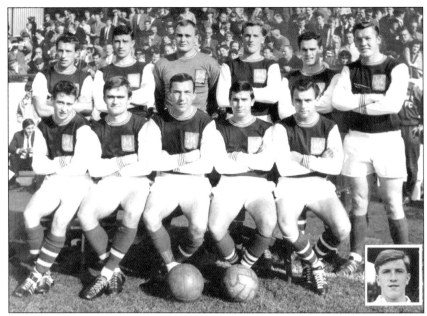

The Cobblers top Division Two in October 1964. Back: Mike Everitt, Derek Leck, Bryan Harvey, Terry Branston, Joe Kiernan, Charlie Livesey. Front: Harry Walden, Bobby Hunt, Theo Foley, Brian Etheridge, Tommy Robson. (Inset, Bobby Brown)

Skipper Wilf 'Tim' McCoy leads out Maurice Candlin, Eddie 'Spud' Murphy and Dave Smith at the County Ground in August 1949 for a match with Newport County

Bryan Harvey saves from Manchester United's John Connelly (No 7)
during the 1-1 draw at the County Ground in August 1965

Fred Pickering makes it 2-1 for Everton in the Division One opener
at Goodison Park in August 1965

Martin Chivers of Southampton sends a header past Terry Branston
at The Dell in September 1964

Returning home … Ken Leek had a
second spell with the Cobblers after
playing for Leicester City, Newcastle
United and Birmingham City, and is
seen here putting pen to paper,
watched by secretary Ray Osborne
and manager Dave Bowen

Ian St John's header past an airborne Graham Carr gives Liverpool the lead in the 0-5
thrashing at Anfield in November 1965

The Cobblers squad of 1961-62 which finished eighth in Division Three

Skipper Theo Foley is watched in training by Terry Branston and Dave Bowen

Foley the chef … Theo Foley is pictured with the singer Ruby Murray at the opening of Foley's Take-N-Bake pie and chip shop in Northampton

West Brom's Clive Clark swivels to equalise against the Cobblers
at the Hawthorns in February 1966

The dread moment ... Steve Earle wheels
away in delight after completing his hat-
trick to virtually condemn the Cobblers to
relegation in Fulham's 4-2 win at the
County Ground in April 1966

Bryan Harvey and Graham Carr help keep the predatory George Best at bay during the 1-1 draw with Manchester United in August 1966

Welcome to the big time … Cobblers supporters probably need a route map to find Highbury in September 1965

ARSENAL FOOTBALL CLUB LTD.

ARSENAL STADIUM
HIGHBURY, N.5

Football League, Div. 1.

ARSENAL
v.

NORTHAMPTON TOWN
TUESDAY, 28th SEPT., 1965

Kick off 7.30 p.m.

Reserved Seat

12/6

Issued subject to conditions on reverse

THIS PORTION TO BE RETAINED

Nº 195

WEST STAND
HIGHBURY HILL
(See Map on back)

BLOCK
Z

ROW
T

SEAT
180

Striker Bobby Hunt heads the Cobblers' second goal at Goodison Park in August 1965

Thanks for the memories. Part of the itinerary of the Cobblers' 1966 German tour

MONDAY, 16th MAY

11.20 Hours. Depart Hanover Airport for Frankfurt. (Flight No. LH.134).

12.30 Hours. ARRIVE FRANKFURT AIRPORT. A coach will convey the party to Ginsheim where Headquarters will be: HOTEL RHEINBLICK. (Tel.: 571).

TUESDAY, 17th MAY

10.00 Hours. Sightseeing Tour of the Opel Car Works at Russelsheim.

WEDNESDAY, 18th MAY

Programme will be announced at breakfast.

THURSDAY, 19th MAY

Programme will be announced at Headquarters.

16.00 Hours. SPORTCLUB OPEL RUSSELSHEIM v. NORTHAMPTON TOWN.

19.00 Hours. Banquet at Hotel Rheinblick.

FRIDAY, 20th MAY

08.15 Hours. Depart Hotel Rheinblick for TRIER, where Headquarters will be: HOTEL DEUTSCHER HOF. (Tel.: 7 33 20).

SATURDAY, 21st MAY

Programme will be announced at breakfast.

18.30 Hours. SPORTVEREIN EINTRACHT TRIER v. NORTHAMPTON TOWN.

SUNDAY, 22nd MAY

07.30 Hours. Depart Headquarters by coach for Frankfurt.

10.45 Hours. Arrive Frankfurt Airport.

11.35 Hours. Depart Frankfurt (Flight No. BEA.603).

12.55 Hours. Arrive London Airport, from which a coach will convey the party to Northampton.

AU REVOIR

AND THANKS FOR THE MEMORIES

Everton's Derek Temple heads for goal during Northampton's First Division baptism at
Goodison Park in August 1965

Roger Hunt fires Liverpool's third
goal in the Cobblers' 0-5 hammering
at Anfield in November 1965

They had said it would never happen, but 21 years before Wimbledon attained such dizzy heights in the face of incredible odds, Bowen's side had performed a trick which was no less dazzling.

Four years earlier they had left Division Four, third in the table behind Peterborough and Crystal Palace. In four more years they would return. For now though, as the roller-coaster pointed its nose skyward, making an outrageously tilted ascent, it was a case of simply sitting back and enjoying the view. Worry about the future later ...

You can't be sure that James Alexander-Gordon was reading the football results which crackled over the radio, or imagine quite how loud the roar sounded on the Portsmouth team bus *en route* to the County Ground. But with due apologies to Swindon, it's nice to imagine a happy reaction to a score which read: Southampton 2 Swindon Town 1. Terry Paine's late winner for the Saints meant Pompey needed just a point from their final game of the season to avoid the drop and relegate Swindon into Division Three. A chance.

However, George Smith's side had won only once away from home all season, losing fourteen out of 21. They had capitulated 0-7 at Ipswich in November, 1-6 at Preston in March, among other fair hidings, and their task was not straightforward. After all, the Cobblers' home record represented a fortress. Still, a draw would do.

The contest had stature enough, but it also provided the stage for an emotional farewell to that old Pompey stalwart and England international Jimmy Dickinson on his fortieth birthday. Dickinson, who had won 48 caps for England between 1949-56 and played in the infamous 0-1 World Cup defeat by the USA in 1950, was bowing out after his 764th league appearance for Portsmouth. He cut a cake on the pitch before the game, while both teams seemed to have an inkling that the cases of champagne in the dressing room would be needed later.

A generation before the advent of Sky television cameras, a crowd of 20,660 packed into the County Ground to toast the mighty home achievement and cheer the local heroes and Dickinson's braves onto the field. Nowadays, of course, it wouldn't be allowed. The apparent licence to contrive a result would be leapt upon from a great height by FA headquarters. This match should surely have kicked off at 3pm, at the same time as the one at The Dell.

Only a month earlier the Cobblers had experimented with Saturday night football, when they defeated Rotherham 1-0 at home with a Bobby Brown goal. That allowed fans the chance to watch Jay Trump deny the bold top weight Freddie in the Grand National in the hands of American amateur Mr (Tommy) Crompton Smith, before striking out for the

County Ground. A year later the home local derby with Leicester City was also played in the afternoon, after the thrills and spills of Aintree in the afternoon.

The Portsmouth match was one of those occasions when the quality of football was incidental to the outcome. Managers are oft-quoted as saying: 'It's the result that counts.' On this night, it certainly meant a lot to Portsmouth, and while Northampton's surreal elevation would not have been affected by a 0-1 loss, there was always that proud home record to preserve.

And for 77 minutes, all went smoothly to plan. Very little happened. History has not recorded whether any Swindon fans were present on this occasion, but had the odd one shuffled onto the Spion Kop at any point, he (or she) would surely have been in a sombre mood, darkening still further as the evening went on. In fact Portsmouth came closest to scoring when Johnny 'Flash' Gordon crashed a volley from thirty yards which Harvey tipped against the crossbar.

Then, for Portsmouth, disaster. Foley took a free-kick and, when Gordon and Harris collided, the former's attempted clearing header flew past John Armstrong to give the home side a lead they scarcely needed or deserved.

Catastrophe for Gordon, who recalled in Peter Jeffs' biography of Dickinson: 'I thought the Pompey supporters would blame me for the rest of their lives if we had lost by that goal. Had we lost, I would have walked home from Northampton and given up the game.'

Fate's hand had played an unlikely card, but suddenly at last, there was a sense of urgency to proceedings. In a rip-roaring finale, parity was restored through Pompey full-back Alex Wilson. Harvey recalled a muttered conversation with inside-forward 'Harry' Harris – who played nearly 400 times for Pompey – as they waited for the fateful corner to come over. 'I never liked conceding goals and it was a personal affront against me if someone did,' said Harvey. 'We had our unbeaten home record to consider but Harris said something like "Come on, you can let one in," to which I replied "if you want to take me out, you can do." But in the end he just obstructed me and from the melee they equalised.'

It mattered not that Wilson had scored only one league goal in more than 250 league appearances for Pompey when his shot took a deflection to bobble past Harvey. When the final whistle was blown a few minutes later, the score was still 1-1. Swindon were down, Portsmouth were saved, but the Cobblers were going up.

CHAPTER SIX

CHEESE WEDGES, LEEK & WEST HAM

It is better to be born lucky than rich, although Dave Bowen would have questioned the sentiment as the Cobblers prepared for Division One. Both assets at once are indeed an advantage. So much of life rests on fortune and the timing of key events. Northampton climbed onto football's top rung with a reputation for hard work, employing a shrewd manager but also being paupers and having a ground more suited to the murkier backwaters from which they had risen. Their manager was so shrewd he rarely signed players near Abington Avenue, preferring a fancy hotel on the edge or centre of town, or as Bowen liked to quip, with the lights switched off. If someone coughed in his office, an inch of dust used to fall from the sloping ceiling, hardly a selling point for the intended recruit and his wife (far more important than agents in those days).

Unreality was the overwhelming sensation during the summer of 1965. Joe Kiernan recalled with a shaking sense of disbelief the first time they saw the printed fixture card with Everton (away) and Arsenal and Manchester United at home in the first eight days of the great adventure. Skipper Theo Foley said: 'When the fixtures came out I was still looking for us in Division Two.'

Kiernan's footballing idol was Denis Law, who would have similar feelings of incredulity, although his misgivings concerned the County Ground with its three sides and ramshackle roofing. Someone thoughtfully placed a sign which read: 'This Way Denis Law' over the players' entrance for that first Saturday home game on 28 August. Law was believed to be less than fully fit after returning from injury and immediate impressions around him were not inspiring.

There's another tale of morbid, tragic irony concerning those 'pinch me, I think I'm dreaming' days of August. That of the season ticket holder who took his seat in the stand for the Wednesday night fixture with Arsenal before turning to his companion remarking: 'I never thought I'd see the day when Cobblers tickets were sold on the black market.' Within minutes he was dead in his seat, having suffered a heart attack. I know this to be true, as I've spoken to the man who inherited his ticket.

The Cobblers board, now headed by Ted Buller – after the death of coach firm businessman Fred York in March – did their best to adopt a professional stance when faced with the new challenge. Sadly though, good intentions didn't involve a substantial pot of money for Bowen, who used to refer to the inadequate £25,000 he was offered for team strengthening before the much-awaited kick-off on 21 August.

Even on that day at Everton, the club's mindset was almost still locked in Division Three (South), a division which had qualified for dinosaur status seven years earlier. The lavish boardrooms of Goodison Park, Old Trafford, Anfield and Highbury were a far cry from the County Ground with its poky, dark, cave-like interiors. 'Tea and biscuits, Mr Busby? Only one of the custard creams if you don't mind … we've got West Brom coming in a fortnight.'

This was not a rich club, and however laudable it seemed to reward players who had won promotion from Division Two, the absence of pre-season signings of note was naïve, given the challenges which lay ahead. Entering the equivalent of the lions' den, the Cobblers had only five players with any experience in the top league – Bryan Harvey, Ken Leek, Bobby Brown, Charlie Livesey and Mike Everitt.

Goalkeeper Harvey began his career at Wisbech and played eighty times for Newcastle between 1958-60 under Charlie Mitten before moving to Blackpool, where he spent two seasons as an understudy to Tony Waiters, who won five England caps. Harvey said: 'I should have gone from Newcastle to West Ham for £10,000 but three weeks before I was due to sign, I broke a toe. I moved to Blackpool after coming back from playing in the United States during the summer. Blackpool had just sold Gordon West to Everton, but I only played in the first team when Tony was injured, and had between 20-30 games in all. They had plenty of talent at the time with England Under-23 internationals such as Jimmy Armfield, Roy Parry and Ray Charnley.'

Everitt and Brown had both tasted life in Division One, playing nine times each for Arsenal and Fulham respectively. Everitt's background was with Essex Schoolboys, where he played with Bobby Hunt, before joining Arsenal from school in 1957, signing professional the following year. He made his debut against Fulham in April 1960 and notched his only Gunners' goal in the second match of the next season, a 1-0 home win over Preston. When he lined up at Goodison alongside Branston and Lines, all three had played in all four divisions for the Cobblers, a select club which Leck joined on the following Wednesday.

Amateur status allowed Brown to play for England at the Rome Olympics in 1960, while his Fulham baptism was in October of that year, which resulted in a 3-0 victory at Bolton Wanderers inspired by Graham Leggat's hat-trick. Brown's three Division One goals before joining the Cobblers came with a double in a 4-4 draw against Manchester United, and a Christmas Eve strike in a 2-3 defeat at Manchester City. Brown recalled: 'I remember deliberately letting the ball run past me in the warm-up to the Manchester United game at Craven Cottage so I could chase it and go near to Bobby Charlton.' Surely, this was akin to the Cobblers' own feeling of awe when suddenly pitched in among so many legends.

At various stages along the line, Northampton failed in attempts to sign Colin Bell (Bury), Mike Summerbee (Swindon), Charlie Cooke (Aberdeen and Dundee), Ian Hamilton (Hibernian) and Alex Stepney (Millwall and Chelsea) before they became stars in their own right. It probably didn't help that Bell and Summerbee had played at the County Ground, and both went on to notable success at Manchester City, under the guiding hand of Bowen's great mate Joe Mercer.

The board now comprised Buller, Eric Northover, Bob Brett, Reggie Saunders, Archie Whatton, Wally Penn and Con Wilson, although none possessed the wealth needed to trouble football's hierarchy. They were a well-meaning and hard-working bunch, caught out by the sudden swift tide. Penn and Brett were farmers, Wilson a builder, Buller dealt in the leather trade, Northover ran a chemist's shop, and Whatton a timber merchants at Roade. Saunders' establishment was the most popular of the lot, as the Cromwell Cottage restaurant at Kislingbury was a haven for Northampton diners intent on a good night out.

Secretary Ray Osborne exerted some influence, having worked at the FA before joining the club in 1960 (he ran a tobacconists in the town after leaving in 1967) and it was largely through his dealing that the club's pre-season fixture list had a glamorous look. Bowen ensured Arsenal had been the visitors for the club's official floodlight opening match on 10 October 1960, but Osborne's network helped explore new, wider, and in some case dubious horizons.

In May, a party of 24 embarked on a ten-day tour of Czechoslovakia, which involved a plane-landing from hell, long, uncomfortable train journeys, cold soup with raw eggs, thick undrinkable coffee, and matches with Koskis (2-2) and Pardubice (1-1), Povaszka Bystricas (1-0), and a 2-3 defeat by Dukla Prague.

The football at least was respectable. In Prague – where the sight of a tank on the programme cover and the introduction to various Russian Army officials on a snow-covered pitch (Yuri Gagarin was at the Koskis match) – the Cobblers played the diplomatic card to lose 2-3, fighting back from 0-3 down with goals by Brown and an own-goal, after Lines and Leek came on at half-time as inside-forwards.

Lines said: 'Dukla Prague were a decent Army side and we understood that, under the Communist regime, if other clubs had decent players they were promptly called up, so they could sign for them. I played in all the matches on the trip after that and scored a couple of goals. After at least two matches there were stage-endings in the Berlin-Prague-Warsaw cycle race and we were told by our Czech guide at one of them that a Russian rider in front had deliberately been routed in the wrong direction by a lead motorcyclist so a Czech rider could win.

'The only meat we saw during the trip was veal except when we visited the British Embassy where we spent a very enjoyable evening. Nothing had been arranged. A group of us bumped into someone while we were walking around Prague and we were offered an invitation, with Theo handling the negotiations. The embassy people said they were normally notified by clubs who were out there. Another club, I think it was Derby, were in Prague at the same time and did this – but they knew nothing about us being there. I remember Dave Bowen wasn't happy when we went along. Later when we played at Pardubice we stayed in accommodation no better than workers hostels and there was a protest until we were found something better. The train journey back from there was a long slog as we were flying home the next day. Ten days was probably too long.'

Chronicle & Echo reporter Mike Beesley was at Heathrow Airport to greet the returning European travellers, but reported seeing sheepish white faces. The Czech aircraft only completed its journey after a second descent, the first having been aborted in filthy, wet conditions. The plane spent another five minutes circling the skies. 'They told us these planes were made so they could easily be converted into bombers, and a week or so later one of them ended in a field at the end of the runway although no-one was hurt,' said Lines.

There must have been a flashpoint in Bowen's mind about the Munich Air disaster of 1958. He had played against the Busby Babes five days earlier at Highbury. As far as the Cobblers were concerned – and after the Plymouth flight experience a month earlier – it seemed good reason not to entertain notions of European qualification.

Beesley was present at the 2-2 draw in Rapid Vienna on 13 August, six days after Bowen's side had returned triumphant from Scotland with the Paisley Cup after a 2-0 win over St Mirren. Second-half goals by Robson and Livesey did the trick, although Archie Gemmill broke his leg in a collision with Leck. As film critic on the *Echo*, Beesley was enraptured by the Austrian city: 'I had been a big fan of the Orson Welles film, *The Third Man*, with the famous fairground scene and remember being awestruck by the fact the stadium backed onto that.'

Beesley filed his report under the headline 'Viennese Crowd Rose To Bowen's Boys', the first word inevitably being 'Wunderbar!' The Cobblers led 2-1 at half-time, coming from behind with goals by Hunt and winger Ronnie Walton, who would join Crewe in October, although the greater part of his league career consisted of ten years with Aldershot, punctuated by a year at Cambridge.

Victory in Vienna might have been clinched if Kiernan's free-kick had been allowed to stand early in the second period. Even so, the draw was greeted back home with the conviction that the Cobblers could hold their own, only for a 1-6 'friendly' defeat at Leicester to dampen optimism. Branston damaged his ankle tripping over a coping stone on the side of the pitch, placing his return in doubt after his 1964-65 campaign had been curtailed by his cartilage operation. Not surprisingly, his injury earned far fewer column injuries in the national press than the broken wrist suffered by Gordon Banks, which sidelined the England goalkeeper for the first nine weeks of the World Cup season.

Branston's ankle presented not the only selection problem ahead of the historic trip to Everton. Don Martin's jaw had been fractured in training, and he was to miss the first eight games, while Leck was suspended after his sending-off at Plymouth in April.

Yet it was a proud day for Foley, leading the team out at Goodison Park, ten years after the Dublin-born right-back had made his Exeter debut against Norwich as a raw teenager after moving across the waters from Home Farm. 'Everybody realised it was a dream come true for us to play in Division One,' he said.

Bowen gambled on Branston's fitness and although the decision backfired, his side were just 21 minutes from a 1-1 draw when the house of cards collapsed. It was the first occasion substitutes had been allowed, initially only for injuries, and Carr sat on the Northampton bench, as insurance to cover the defensive uncertainty.

England manager Alf Ramsey was among the 48,489 who witnessed Scottish international Alex Young put Harry Catterick's men 1-0 up. Harvey failed to hold Alex Scott's shot, after the outside-right had swapped passes with full-back Tommy Wright.

However, that landmark in Northampton history, a first ever goal at the top level, was not long in coming. The instigator was Kiernan with an incisive ball to Hunt, who passed to Brown. Although the striker's shot was miscued, it wrong-footed Gordon West in the Everton goal.

The Cobblers survived sustained pressure and a host of Everton chances, but Branston's ankle gave way midway through the second half when he landed awkwardly after challenging for a high ball. Kurila was booked for a foul on Colin Harvey. The free-kick bounced off Derek Temple's knee and fell to Fred Pickering, who restored the lead.

Carr stayed on the bench as Branston hobbled on, and Temple made it 3-1. Hunt pulled a goal back with a header, but Pickering and Temple helped themselves to another one apiece. It ended 5-2.

Elsewhere, Fulham – who would prove the Cobblers' nemesis – drew 2-2 at Blackpool, where Northampton's season would end in April. Leicester were beaten 1-3 at home by champions-to-be Liverpool, while Manchester United defeated Sheffield Wednesday 1-0. Arsenal beat Stoke 2-1, but goalkeeper Jim Furnell was injured. This allowed Bob Wilson to replace him at the County Ground on the Wednesday night, when the future TV pundit faced up to his old England amateur teammate Brown.

With the extent of Branston's injury apparent, Carr and Leck were brought in. Kurila was the other man to stand down, while Cockcroft became the first Cobblers No 12 to be used. He replaced Everitt, hurt during a collision with Dave Court in the first minute, but who soldiered on for another 36 minutes.

By that time the Cobblers were behind. Harvey dropped a George Armstrong shot, allowing Tommy Baldwin to fire home, but twelve minutes after the break good work by Kiernan and Robson allowed Brown to head the equaliser. Victory might even have been won, with Carr's run taking him past a line of Arsenal defenders before his fierce shot tested Wilson, while Brown's header came back off the base of a post.

The eleven which finished the Arsenal game were retained three days later against Manchester United, and came from behind to earn another 1-1 draw. The Cobblers side might have been put together for £12,000 while Matt Busby's line-up cost £300,000, but no matter. United looked fallible when losing 2-4 at Nottingham Forest on the Tuesday, and their fans were in for another disappointing afternoon, a small percentage of them venting their frustration on the Spread Eagle pub in the town, on which they carried out their own brand of interior re-design.

The day was especially memorable for Kiernan, whose wife Pat had given birth to their first child Michelle, during the early hours of Saturday morning. He had spent the night at the home of Kurila and his wife Nan so he could be closer to the hospital and the ground.

Kiernan recalled: 'On the Friday night we were ringing the hospital from a phone box 300 yards away from where the Kurilas lived but on the Saturday morning Nan woke me up around 7am and said "congratulations, you've become a father". I said "how the hell do you know" and it turned out she couldn't sleep and had been down the road to the phone box about three times in the night. I went to the hospital to see them before going home to get some sleep to freshen myself up for the game, as I had something of a broken night.'

Cobblers fans quickly learned that the old quip which questioned the kick-off time ('What time can you get here?') no longer applied in Division One. The roads around the County Ground became congested from midday and spectators had to stand like squashed sardines from 1pm if they were to get a clear view from the Hotel End or Spion Kop terracing. The crowd, 21,245, was the club's biggest ever league gate, passing the 21,102 who had seen Plymouth in 1929, when the Cobblers had finished fourth to Argyle in Division Three (South).

The crush heading for the United game compounded Kiernan's problems: 'I slept through my alarm and didn't wake up until 1.15pm, thinking "Jesus Christ, I'm going to struggle to get there in time". I had to drive across town from New Duston (nearly five miles). Because of the crowd it was 2.20pm by the time I had parked on the cricket side and was rushing across the pitch to the dressing rooms thinking that Dave Bowen was going to go mad at me. I remember a copper saying "Bloody Hell, Joe are you playing today?" to which I replied "I hope so". Someone had put out over the tannoy that I had become a father and the Hotel End was in full voice singing "e-i-addio, Joe is a Daddio". In the dressing room I asked someone if Denis Law was playing, to which they said "yes". I was so pleased as Manchester United were my favourite team and Denis Law was my idol.'

As the match neared its conclusion, with the Cobblers trailing to a John Connolly goal, it might have been the Catholic faith shared by Kiernan and Foley that saved the day. Kiernan said: 'I remember thinking, "please God, this has been such a perfect day, now let us get something out of it," and then Bobby Hunt blasted one in from twenty yards to earn us a point. It really was the perfect day.'

It was quickly apparent that dredging every ounce of effort to match Arsenal and Manchester United would not solve the looming headaches. With marked understatement, Bowen muttered after the United game: 'It's a different world, this,' and so it was to prove. The next two matches brought defeats, and the Cobblers back down to earth. A 0-2 loss at Newcastle was followed by a 1-4 drubbing at Burnley.

The Newcastle game was a personal tragedy for Harvey, whose blunder shortly after half-time gifted the Geordies the lead. In attempting to boot a Foley back-pass into touch, he gifted the ball to Alan Suddick who slotted it home. Although the Cobblers matched their opponents and had as many chances, they fell 0-2 behind when Dave Hilley's cross from the right bounced off Carr's legs to George Cummings.

The Rolling Stones' *I Can't Get No Satisfaction* would soon to be No 1 in the charts, and even if the Cobblers players didn't belt out their own version on the team coach coming back from Burnley on the Tuesday, it would have been an appropriate rallying call.

By contrast, Harvey had received a standing ovation at half-time at Turf Moor after performing heroics and only conceding a Foley own-goal for his old club. Although Livesey was on target, Kiernan's early second-half injury was the final nail in that night's coffin.

The Cobblers had sunk to the foot of Division One on the Monday, with Blackpool's 4-0 win over Leicester, but at least Bowen's men had the chance to 'get one in early' themselves on the Friday evening with the visit of free-scoring West Brom.

Often when delving into Cobblers players' pasts, you feel that many fulfilled their careers to provide questions for those orange cheese wedges which slot into the wheels on a Trivial Pursuit game board.

Question: Who was the first player to score for the same club in all four divisions? Answer: Barry Lines. Question: Who was the first player to score in the newly created Division Four in 1958? Answer: Alan Woan (in the first minute at Port Vale). Question: Which Cobblers player scored in every round of the FA Cup for Leicester City in 1960-61, yet was dropped for the final? Answer: Ken Leek.

Theo Foley's bid to qualify for the trivia game, by later coaching or managing at ten different London clubs (including Dartford and Dulwich as well as Arsenal and Tottenham), and Frank Large's feat in playing for nine clubs and being transferred ten times (three spells at Northampton), count merely as gallant failures in this reckoning.

So the 3-4 defeat by West Brom might have left the Cobblers rooted to the foot of the table, but at least it scored heavily for entertainment, while giving Lines his niche in the history books.

Lines, an outside-left, or occasional inside-forward, made all of his 266 league appearances for Northampton between 1960-69. He deserves recognition for loyalty which also extended to his home town, which he has never left. For Branston at Rugby, read Lines at Bletchley. He also provides a link with Cobblers sides of the early '50s, playing as he did in the same Bletchley side as goalkeeper William 'Jack' Ansell who made 131 league appearances for Northampton between 1947-51 and acted as the scout who first alerted Bowen to Lines' potential.

In the twelfth minute against West Brom, Foley sent Billy Best away down the right. Best's cross was headed in by Lines. Sadly, the Cobblers were 0-2 down at the time, with Jeff Astle having scored the first of his hat-trick and Bobby Hope getting a second. Robson tied it up at 2-2 and added another near the end, but this was really Astle's night, as he took his tally to nine goals in a season which was less than three weeks old.

Matters failed to improve with a 1-2 home defeat by Burnley the following Wednesday, a match put back 24 hours to avoid a clash with Leicester's 0-3 defeat by Blackpool. Robson's thirty-yard shot on the turn was a cracker, but ultimately it counted for little.

A sequence of four draws served merely to heighten the sense of winless frustration, although after the first, at Nottingham Forest, Blackburn were defeated 1-0 at Ewood Park in the second round of the League Cup. The outstanding Kiernan teed up Everitt for the goal. In the *Chronicle & Echo*, Mike Beesley wrote: 'Kiernan has played many fine games for the Cobblers in the past 12 months, but never has he been more destructive in defence and more constructive in attack.'

At the City Ground, the consolation of a first away point was a skinny one, given the controversial nature of Mike Kear's last-minute Forest equaliser after a goalmouth scramble, one he later admitted had been assisted with a hand. That match was important for Vic Cockcroft, whose first and last league goal in 87 shows for Northampton and Rochdale was the volley from a Foley cross which for so long appeared to be settling Northampton's first win.

Cockcroft was nicknamed 'Z-Victor-One' by teammates on account of his dapper appearance in blazer and smart ties, which gave him the appearance of an airline pilot. He still managed to play in every division of the league for his two clubs after arriving at the County Ground in 1962 from Wolves, at which time he became an England youth international alongside Geoff Hurst, Nobby Stiles and Alan Hinton.

Everitt's League Cup winner at Blackburn triggered further stalemates with Sheffield Wednesday (0-0) – where only Carr and Lines stood out for the Cobblers in a contest which degenerated into a second-half farce amid torrential rain – and the return 1-1 at Arsenal, where Hall, making only his second appearance in the top flight, scored with a classic header from a Kiernan cross. That goal came shortly after John Radford had touched home a George Armstrong cross to give Arsenal the lead. Hall then had a goal disallowed, as Robson had over-stepped a line before crossing. Late on, the ex-England youth international smashed a shot which just skimmed wide. In the end, the shrill whistles of the Arsenal fans baying for the end gave the Cobblers' travelling faithful a memorable night in the city.

The 1-1 draw at Leicester was another game which could have been won, although the unbeaten run now stretched to five games. Branston made his return, coming on as a substitute for groin-strain victim Kurila. Some 8,000 Cobblers fans travelled nose to tail in their motor cars to Filbert Street, where they saw Banks (recovered from his wrist injury) pull off fine saves from Robson and Hall, before being beaten by Foley's penalty, after John Sjoberg had brought down Walden.

Crowd trouble made national headlines on 9 October, with arrests at the Lancashire derby between Burnley and Blackburn (which the visitors astonishingly won 4-1) while club windows were stoned and broken after Manchester United's 2-0 win over Liverpool. Liverpool had yet to assert themselves, and it was the Cobblers' visitors that day, Sheffield United, who arrived and departed as Division One leaders, the fourth team to claim top spot, in the wake of Tottenham, West Brom and Burnley.

Not that the County Ground escaped all aggravation. Referee Burns had to alert police to troublemakers behind the Hotel End goal after ex-England goalkeeper Alan Hodgkinson had been pelted with apple cores. However, note that these were cores, rather than apples, proving again that Northampton supporters are usually peckish, and have always being fully aware of the nutritional value of fruit.

Was this the soft belly of hooliganism? Somehow I struggle to accept this issue existed at all in the '60s, and much of the blame can be laid squarely at the door of a letter I once read in a Chelsea v Liverpool programme that season. In it, the author, a Mr Kevin Ryan, expressed heartfelt thanks to the Chelsea fan who had returned his library ticket after the recent Blackpool clash. He then seemed to use this as a platform to embrace the whole of the Shed End and concluding (somewhat sweepingly) that they were a thoroughly decent lot. Imagine all this today!

There was no doubting where Bowen's allegiances lay, as he signed a new five-year contract on 5 October, although it failed to bring an instant response on the pitch. The Sheffield United loss was followed by a 0-5 hammering at Fulham in the third round of the League Cup, and a 1-6 mauling at Leeds, after Billy Best had put the visitors in front.

After the Fulham game, that respected national scribe Alan Hubbard wrote: 'It seems to be not a question of what is going wrong with Northampton, but of why is nothing going right. Individually they are obviously a side with considerable talent. Why else would this match have attracted such astute observers as Billy Nicholson, manager of Spurs? He was, I believe, keeping a careful eye on Joe Kiernan who is not only playing like Jim Baxter but beginning to look like him as well.'

Billy Best's flirtation with Division One was to prove brief, but the next season he scored ten league and cup goals in 22 appearances before joining Southend, where he assumed legendary status, netting 123 goals over five seasons. He then enjoyed a second promotion back with the Cobblers, alongside Hall. Best once bagged a hat-trick for Southend inside four minutes against Brentwood during a 10-1 FA Cup demolition, in which he scored the last five, admitting: 'We were 5-0 up and I didn't think it was my night.'

Mind you, it almost ended before it began for Best. After scoring on his Cobblers debut during a 3-0 home win over Norwich in September 1963 ('Kevin Keelan punched out a corner and I discovered I could kick with my left foot as well') Best said: 'The next morning I was so anxious to buy a paper over the road from where I was staying at the Old Black Lion that I nearly stepped in front of a car. I played in the next match at Manchester City. All I remember that day was stripping off on the team coach so we could be ready for the kick off.'

If Best and Hall were two examples of 'two-stop' Northampton strikers who experienced better fortune later on, Ken Leek's second spell with Northampton would seem to justify the 'never go back' adage, were it not for the evidence of 23 October 1965, when the Cobblers finally notched a first league win in Division One.

Try Welsh rarebit for a fuller flavour? Bowen was still manfully juggling his club and country duties and it was only natural he should be unable to resist fellow patriots Leek and Graham Moore, who would arrive in December, during his never-ending spin of front men. The pair never played in the same Northampton team but teamed up in a red shirt, often in direct competition for places, the best example coming in Sao Paulo in 1962 when Leek was a second-half substitute for Moore, scoring the Welsh goal in a 1-3 defeat by Brazil.

Leek had joined the Cobblers groundstaff as a seventeen-year-old in 1952, and scored one of the goals which stunned Bowen and his Arsenal team in the 1958 FA Cup giantkilling. He then made the short hop up the A50 to join Leicester, who had been Division Two champions in 1956-57. He returned to the County Ground as a 29-year-old in 1964, having further enjoyed a fulsome career with Newcastle and Birmingham, with whom he won a League Cup winners' medal.

Originally from Ynysbwl in the Rhondda Valley, Leek had proved a close ally to Bowen on the national stage, the pair going back to their country's build-up to the World Cup in Sweden in 1958. He won thirteen caps, the last of them in Greece in a World Cup qualifier while on the Cobblers books in 1965, scoring five times in all for his country.

Leek's call-up to the seventeen-strong Welsh squad in 1958 had come after an injury to Blackburn's Roy Vernon. He had scored in a shock 2-1 Under-23 international against an England team including Brian Clough and Jimmy Greaves at Wrexham in April, and he was ready for the challenge. Preparations for the World Cup saw Leek and Bowen travel from Northampton to meet the rest of the squad in London.

'We spent a week training there and a lot of the time we were on Hyde Park. To loosen up we used to run around the park and then it was coats down on the ground for goals,' said Leek.

Welsh performances in Sweden exceeded all expectations. Draws with Hungary, Mexico and Sweden earned a play-off with Hungary which Wales won 2-1. The run came to an end in the quarter-finals, when they were beaten 0-1 by eventual winners Brazil in Gothenberg. Legendary striker John Charles was absent through injury, but the Welsh, led magnificently by Bowen, held out until a late shot by Pele was deflected past Jack Kelsey by Stuart Williams.

Leek, a fascinated spectator in all this, observed Bowen as the player and gifted wing half … but also the manager in the moulding. He reflected: 'Players tended to go around in groups of three or four but Dave was a man apart. He was very close to Jimmy Murphy the manager. They kept their own counsel and you almost think now that he was being groomed for the role.'

Wherever Leek went he scored goals, and his overall Northampton record bears testimony to this with 33 in 93 league and cup shows. As a centre-forward or inside-right for Leicester, he was prolific, after netting on his debut in a 2-0 win over Everton. In 1960-61 he bagged 25, including the seven which helped take The Foxes to Wembley, where they lost 0-2 to Tottenham in Spurs' double-winning year.

For sheer 'tales of the unexpected', here lies the story to which Leek is most closely bound. His omission by Matt Gillies in the Cup final would have given the headline writers in *The Sun* material for a week in these times of modern 'culture'. The fact he went on to score twice in the first leg of the 1963 League Cup final for Birmingham City, as they beat fierce rivals Aston Villa 3-1 (the second leg was drawn 0-0) acted as some consolation.

No one is suggesting Leek's performance for Northampton against West Ham on that fateful day was anything out of the ordinary, but goalscorers make the difference, and that was exactly what happened on this occasion. England captain Bobby Moore was among those most bitter at the first-half decision of Sheffield referee David Payne to award the Cobblers a penalty, after Dennis Burnett brought down Bobby Hunt. Foley tucked away the spot-kick, only for West Ham to equalise shortly after half-time when Ken Brown headed in a John Sissons corner. Leek though, had the last laugh. Ten minutes from the end his cheeky back-flick converted a Hunt cross and the majority of the 15,367 crowd breathed a collective sigh of relief.

CHAPTER SEVEN

CLIMBING THE SLIPPERY POLE

If the Cobblers believed that one victory over West Ham would establish them overnight as a club with Division One credibility, they were mistaken. Still, the Hammers were a notable first scalp on their string. The 1964 FA Cup winners had followed up with the European Cup-Winners' Cup the following season and included all three of their soon-to-be England World Cup winners – Bobby Moore, Martin Peters and Geoff Hurst – in both games with Bowen's men.

Despite the briefness of the Division One encounter, it is still refreshing at times to sit back and remind yourself that Northampton have never lost to West Ham, Arsenal, Aston Villa, Nottingham Forest or Leicester in the league – this includes a win and three draws with Forest in Division Three (South) between 1949-51. Mind you, on one side of the fence, we appear to have spent an awful long time since avoiding them, while on the other, they appear strangely reluctant to find us to try to set the record straight.

Centre-half Graham Carr celebrated his 21st birthday two days after the Hammers win, a game which reporter Beesley curiously described as 'ranging between the thrilling and the monotonous'. Celebrations were in order, and the Saturday night was spent by the players toasting both landmarks at the local Sywell Airport Motel, a popular nightspot at the time. No surprises then, that Bowen's men felt it was time for take-off …

Carr had played with Tommy Robson in his native North East for Newcastle junior side Corinthians before he first came to Northampton in August 1962. He had been spotted by the club's North-East scout Jack Patterson, the father of their former player Ron. Like teammates such as Robson, Jim Hall, Don Martin, Brian Etheridge and Colin Sharpe, Carr was an England youth international and in October 1965 he seemed to have the world at his feet.

Many years later Carr would reflect on a Northampton playing career which ended in 1968 with the side back in Division Three before the switch to such outposts as York and Bradford Park Avenue. 'Something must have gone wrong, somewhere,' he mused.

Carr had patiently bided his time to earn first-team recognition, making a solitary appearance in both 1962-63 and the following season, at Bournemouth and Southampton, before Branston's cartilage operation had opened doors for him at the back end of 1964-65.

Partly due to his concern with keeping a tighter ship in Division One, Bowen gradually began to lose faith with Derek Leck, who was never as keen on the defensive part of his wing-half duties as when foraging forward to support the attack, so even the gradual return of Branston to full fitness did not oust Carr from the side.

A fiery competitor both on and off the field, Carr seemed the least likely of that Cobblers squad to later become a manager, yet the wayward streak which dogged him during his playing days turned to his advantage once he sat on the other side of the desk, notably when steering the Cobblers to the Division Four title in 1986-87. Having fallen foul of the rules himself, he knew all the dodges players could invent and earned their respect. He then performed scouting jobs for the likes of Coventry, Tottenham and Manchester City, and along with Foley has always been 'the network man' in the Cobblers Old Boys chain.

As a player, Carr prompted an assessment from goalkeeper Harvey that he was an inch or two short of being a top quality centre-half, but there was no question of his loyalty as a fighting young buck. Attributed with the quote: 'I'll argue with anyone who says Northampton are not a good side!' in a souvenir promotion programme, there would surely have been few takers, considering the reputation he enjoyed.

However, Carr combined that combative edge with a wicked sense of humour. It appears in keeping that one of his sons, Alan, has carved out a career as a stand-up comedian with a growing list of national television and club credits after being propelled to fame by winning a best new BBC talent award at the Edinburgh Festival.

In the days when, as a local reporter, I used to visit the upstairs offices at 195 Abington Avenue in the late 1980s, you could never be certain of Carr's mood. Would it be the strict disciplinarian or the party animal? I infinitely preferred the latter. In this frame of mind, he might casually pick up the telephone on his desk while gazing intently across the road to the cricket square, where in high summer a high-ranking executive would be in earnest conversation with a groundsman.

As a master of cunning voice disguise, what followed was a few eloquent words to the cricket club receptionist, after which someone would appear on the balcony to disrupt the debate out in the middle. Then, long before the victim had reached the pavilion, let alone the telephone, England's 'chairman of selectors' had replaced the receiver and burst into laughter with his assembled audience, which might include assistant manager Clive Walker or one of his old buddies from the 1960s days, who had popped in to swap tales when the Geordie was not wheeler-dealing in the transfer market.

Carr could laugh at himself as well as others. On the fateful day of the Fulham defeat he hadn't featured in the first team for over two months. Never a prolific goalscorer (in fact he never hit the target for the Cobblers, though he did at York and Bradford), he netted at Desborough and recalled: 'I was in the third team with the likes of Vic Cockcroft and always remember the *Green 'Un* which described it as one of the best goals ever seen at the Waterworks Field!' Surely this was a case of being in the wrong place at the wrong time.

Another favourite story which summed up the County Ground (definitely still ramshackle in the mid-1980s) concerned a day he was sitting in the portable dug-out on the cricket side. It was just before half-time when veteran odd-job man Harry Warden (not to be confused with '60s winger Walden) poked his head around the side and uttered the immortal words: 'Graham, we've run out of milk!' Welcome to Northampton Town. What would the board of directors have said about a team strategist who disappeared to the Co-op for his two-pinter at 3.40pm on a Saturday afternoon, with his team talk pending?

Bowen was once attributed with the words: 'I love playing with other people's money.' He had to, in order to strengthen his squad. After scoring against West Ham, Ken Leek played in the 0-3 defeat at Sunderland before Bradford City paid out a record fee of £10,000 for him. His near-namesake, Leck's, seven and a half years at the County Ground ended with a £6,000 move to Brighton in November.

Leck was burdened with some unkind nicknames at Northampton, with sections of the crowd calling him 'Daisy'. He was 'Leckeroo' in the dressing room, while Foley ribbed him as 'Phyllis'. But whatever he was labelled, his teammates appreciated what he offered 'box-to-box', covering ground like a bounding kangaroo. Harvey, for one, singled out his talents, while Branston once lost patience and rounded on a critical supporter, snapping: 'Do you honestly suppose the manager has got it wrong so often all these years by picking Derek Leck?'

Popping up in both penalty areas has the additional advantage of making you an oft-photographed player, and it's surprising how often Leck appears on film. Some 268 league and cup appearances and 49 goals pay tribute to his loyalty and eye for goal.

Having players named 'Leck' and 'Leek' in the same side is bound to cause confusion, while also being a sub-editor's nightmare, although it helps that the names are practically unique in English (and Welsh) football history. The pair narrowly missed overlapping in the late 1950s, while playing in the same team just twelve times in 1964-65 and on three occasions in Division One. That fact helped ease the headache a little.

It is an understandable grey area. Perhaps that's why they were sold a month apart, especially when their destinations both began 'Br'. Best to ensure they go to the right grounds, as Brighton and Bradford are poles apart. Both players always shared a passion for 'the gee gees', and to use a racing analogy, it would be like packing off the wrong colts from a stable to run in maiden races at Redcar and Folkestone, only to confuse their passports and discover the problem while unloading their horseboxes some 400 miles away.

The only time I ever pinned down an example of their names getting tangled up, was in the club's own 'Definitive Guide', an otherwise excellent reference, which has Leek wearing the No 10 shirt at Liverpool. The match took place nine days after his sale to Bradford City.

This reveals refreshing honesty on Leck's part, for it is not an obvious move to admit to performing in the 0-5 hammering inflicted on a day Coe performed brilliantly in goal to keep down the score. 'I certainly played at Liverpool,' Leck told me when I queried the point, and there was almost a quiver in his voice as the memories flooded back.

Sunderland had won five out of six at home prior to the Cobblers' visit (drawing the other with Fulham), so it's perhaps not surprising Bowen's men should have come a cropper, especially considering their results when travelling more than sixty miles that season.

With so many snarl-ups on motorway networks, supporters are used to modern day headaches on the roads, but allowing sufficient time to reach a destination was even more of an issue in 1965-66. Billy Best's tale about changing on the team coach before playing at Manchester City was not an isolated case.

The side usually travelled by coach (after all, late chairman Fred York ran a coach business in the town), although the trip to Liverpool was made by train, stirring memories of the massive fans' excursion of 1958. The club's coach driver for many years was Albert Beesley, who as far as I'm aware was no relation.

A glance at the few away matches lost in reaching Division One, and then falling from it, makes interesting reading. In Division Two the six reverses came at Newcastle, Middlesbrough, Plymouth (twice, once in the League Cup), Huddersfield, Southampton and Swindon. All bar the last involved major treks, while in Division One the record was even more remarkable when broken down into regions: the North, the Midlands and London. The results are such that it's a wonder the team coach didn't simply turn back and head home. In eleven matches north of the Midlands, the Cobblers grabbed just a solitary point – at Sheffield United. The other ten were all lost with ten goals scored and 45 conceded.

By contrast, form in the Midlands and London was 'just capital'. Five matches in the Midlands (Stoke City, West Brom, Nottingham Forest, Aston Villa and Leicester) brought a win and three draws, along with a caning at the Victoria Ground. That seems good reason as far as I can see to qualify Stoke as the first outpost in the trek across the frozen northern wastes.

City lights also held few fears for the Cobblers, as a 4-1 win at Fulham (conveniently brushing aside the 0-5 League Cup loss at Craven Cottage), three 1-1 draws (Arsenal, West Ham and Tottenham), and a 0-1 defeat Chelsea serve to testify.

The Sunderland setback ensured there would be no sudden complacency, but the following Saturday brought a second league victory, with Aston Villa sent packing thanks to a 2-1 defeat. Enter Norman Coe and Jim Hall, heroes of the hour. Goalkeeper Coe had not played in the first team for over two years, the 0-3 home defeat by 1963-64 Division Two champions Leeds being his previous show. Harvey was apparently injured at Roker Park, although he later admitted: 'I should have been left out that season before it actually happened.' His deputy came in for a sequence which would extend to fifteen league and cup appearances, and he pulled off some excellent saves that day. The other credits belonged to Hall, whose goals were condensed into a ninety-second period early in the game, although his involvement was curtailed when he departed injured midway through the second half with a hamstring pull, to be replaced by Robson. Hall's opener came after brilliant work by Kiernan, Hunt and Lines, while Walden supplied his second with a cross that the striker cracked home.

Robson was playing for the last time at home in a Cobblers shirt that day, Bowen only using him at Fulham three weeks later so he could flamboyantly appear in the shop window for neighbouring Chelsea spies. They wanted to check he had recovered from flu and could still tie his bootlaces together before sealing a £30,000 deal.

Hall and Robson share a dubious distinction as part of their inclusion in Northampton folklore, as both played most of their careers some forty miles up the road with Peterborough United. It is at moments like this that you feel a duty to remind all and sundry that Posh have never played in the top division of English football.

Hall was sold to the London Road club during 1967-68 and said later: 'Being a local lad (from Kingsthorpe) and playing for Northampton, people always expected things of you. At the Cobblers I never really settled into one position, whereas Peterborough and the manager Norman Rigby persevered with me and did more for my confidence.'

That trust was rewarded with 122 league goals in 302 Peterborough appearances and, more annoyingly, a constant habit of scoring against his home-town club. Copy and headline writers feel spoilt and privileged if this happens once or twice in a career, but seven times? This starts to rub and suggests a certain lack of originality. In Hall's case, coming back to Northampton in the 1970s and playing a key role in the 1975-76 promotion campaign behind Graham Taylor's Lincoln City helped to soften the blow and win back supporters.

Speed was the key to unlocking the success of Robson's career and his lifestyle, even though his switch from Northampton to Chelsea did not prove the springboard to stardom one might have envisaged. This was mainly due to the fact he contracted jaundice, which effectively ended his Stamford Bridge career before it began.

Back at his native Newcastle, where he had moved to recuperate, Robson at last joined the club that had rejected him as a lad. Here though, he added to his collection of more bizarre football injuries by breaking a bone in his foot while gardening, missing a Fairs Cup tie with Feyenoord and in the long term a more productive St James' Park career.

At the Cobblers, Robson often vied with Lines for a place at outside-left, although this dilemma was solved for spells by employing Lines at inside-forward. Attacking full-backs down the left flank, Robson showed greater pace and directness, while also boasting a ferocious shot. Lines was more likely to supply accurate crosses.

Robson's need for speed wasn't just reserved for his time on the pitch. He used to tear around the lake at Oundle on a motor boat named after his first wife 'Josephine' and acted the showman around Northampton in his two-tone blue Ford Zodiac, complete with record player and fitted aerial on the back. On one occasion he proved years ahead of his time with the apparent inclusion of a 'mobile phone'.

Robson explained: 'My first car was an Austin Cambridge which I bought while working for Yorks Coaches in the summer [the Cobblers chairman was Fred York]. I remember holding up the team coach, which stopped outside the Test Centre on its way to Torquay on a Friday afternoon while I passed my test. I also remember having the Zodiac and a policeman stopping all the traffic in Gold Street, which was always full of people on a Saturday afternoon, if we were on our way to a game. But the funniest thing was driving around Northampton one day with Joe Kiernan, Ronnie Walton and Graham Carr. Graham was leaning out of the window and was pretending to talk on a big old-fashioned black phone which was "plugged" with a lead into the ashtray. People were staring in amazement.'

Robson, who made a record 482 league appearances for Posh, scoring 113 goals, holds the distinction of being the last Division One Cobbler to play in the Football League. He was a couple of months short of his 37th birthday when he came on as a substitute during a 1-1 draw with Hereford in 1981. He was another who made an unwelcome habit of scoring against the Cobblers, and on Boxing Day that season had netted in a 3-0 win at London Road, having also scored twice in the Posh's 4-1 FA Cup win at the County Ground.

Against Aston Villa, on the day Hall hit his last Division One goals, Villa's Bobby Park – who would later sign for the Cobblers – pulled a goal back in the second half to set the nerve ends jangling. Park's low shot ensured the Hotel End's supporters endured, rather than lapped up the closing minutes. Referee Stokes played seven minutes of injury-time, during which Villa won three corners, before blowing the final whistle.

Elsewhere, another eventful day saw Arsenal defeat Sheffield United 6-2, while Burnley went top with a 3-1 win over West Ham. Manchester United keeper Harry Gregg was sent off in the 2-2 draw with Blackburn, after which Rovers' coach was stoned leaving the ground. Liverpool notched their fourth away win, scoring twice in the last fifteen minutes at Sheffield Wednesday, bringing the Owls' first home defeat since February, while at Brentford an empty hand-grenade was apparently thrown during their 1-2 home defeat by Millwall in Division Three. The Brentford goalkeeper on that day was none other than the ex-Cobbler custodian Chic Brodie.

The following weekend was equally as dramatic. In the first round of the FA Cup, local minnows Bedford Town and Corby Town advanced with wins over Exeter City (2-1) and Burton Albion (6-3) respectively. Division One brought an end to Spurs' 33-match unbeaten home run, when they lost 2-3 to Sheffield Wednesday. Manchester United won 5-0 at Leicester, while Liverpool hammered the Cobblers 5-0 to stay breathing down the necks of Burnley, who won 4-0 win at Sunderland.

It would be easy to assume from a defeat which equalled the Cobblers' worst margin in Division One that the diminutive Coe had a nightmare at Anfield. In fact he was outstanding, especially in the second half when a tidal wave of Liverpool chances tested him to the limit.

Cobblers players were struck by the training ground nonchalance of Liverpool's opener. Peter Thompson, who gave Foley a testing time all afternoon, found Ian Callaghan out on the right, and his cross was headed home from fourteen yards by Ian St John. Kiernan said: 'The way they walked back to the centre circle was as though they did this sort of thing every minute of their lives.'

Cockcroft brought down Tommy Smith for the second goal, and before the break Hunt had added a third. After half-time Callaghan fired through a ruck of players, but Thompson netted the best of the lot, breaking down the left before cutting inside onto his right foot to drill the ball past Coe.

If Liverpool were the teachers, the Cobblers were at least hard-working pupils who stuck to their task, whatever the gulf in class. On an exacting afternoon, skipper Foley at least kept his sense of humour. After St John had gone close with one of umpteen chances, Foley asked him (not so) politely: 'Why don't you go and have a rest now?'

With Robson set to go to Chelsea, the 0-2 home defeat by Tottenham a week later was notable for the debut of right-winger Joe Broadfoot, after his £27,000 purchase from Ipswich. Broadfoot had scored twelve goals for Ipswich the previous season, including one at the County Ground, but he was unable to make an impression here as Dave Mackay opened the scoring with a 35-yard drive before setting up Frank Saul for the second.

The Cobblers had their moments, with Kiernan hitting a post early on, Martin having a goal disallowed, and Carr seeing a shot kicked off the line, but they didn't do enough to win.

The mood was brighter at Craven Cottage a week later, when the Cobblers hammered Fulham 4-1, even though it wasn't enough to lift them off the foot of the table. In the clubs' first league meeting since 1932, Robson quickly advertised his wares to the watching Chelsea contingent by robbing George Cohen and crossing for Brown to beat Tony Macedo. However, that was to be Macedo's last action, as the Fulham goalkeeper was forced off the field after falling awkwardly under a challenge from Brown. That meant Rodney Marsh taking over between the sticks. Johnny Haynes equalised for Fulham five minutes before the break, but in the Cobblers' next attack, Brown's through ball to Hunt had Marsh firstly coming out and then back-pedalling. The striker finally scored with a shot which went in off Marsh's knee.

Not surprisingly, Bowen's half-time instructions were to 'shoot on sight' and Brown did just that three minutes after the restart, curling in a shot after beating two defenders on a mazy run. Brown's hat-trick was completed with fourteen minutes left when he headed in a Broadfoot cross.

A 2-3 defeat for Fulham at Stoke the next Saturday (4 December), coupled with Blackburn's 1-2 reverse at Sheffield Wednesday, meant that the Cobblers' third home win in four matches lifted them not only off the foot of the table, but out of the relegation zone as well.

Blackpool were the victims, beaten 2-1, and their side included Alan Ball and Jimmy Armfield, playing his first match for three weeks. But it was the Cobblers' recent signing Broadfoot who raised the roof with the first of three goals in an eight-minute spell just after the break, when he collected a pass from Hall before cutting inside to unleash a fierce left-footed shot. When Lines made it 2-0 from an almost identical position four minutes later, the Cobblers had a cushion, only for it to be punctured when Cockcroft brought down Ian Moir. Referee Harry New awarded a penalty which Ball converted. The game's major talking point was a frantic injury-time scramble, during which Branston appeared to clear from behind the goal-line. New was besieged by Blackpool players but refused to allow the 'goal' to stand.

When weighing up the Cobblers' ultimate fate, what happened next was nothing short of a disaster. Given their upturn in fortune and that Blackburn were also embroiled in the relegation struggle, a 1-6 defeat at Ewood Park ought to have been unthinkable.

Yet somehow it happened. The Cobblers' first shot arrived in the 38th minute, by which time they were 0-4 adrift. They trailed 1-5 at the break, with George Jones helping himself to a hat-trick, and were 1-6 down shortly after the interval, when Cockcroft chopped down Mike Ferguson – who had set the fire blazing as early as the seventh minute – allowing outside-left Mike Harrison to convert the penalty.

This turned out to the Cobblers' last game before Christmas, although the scheduled Leeds fixture caused a storm of controversy. Some 3,000 travelling fans had arrived in Northampton when referee Tom Dawes declared the saturated pitch unfit, just an hour before kick-off. Outraged Leeds manager Don Revie said: 'I have seen hundreds of matches played on worse pitches than this.' Leeds' frustration was understandable, as this was their third postponement in a month. Had they been given a sneak preview of what would happen when the fixture eventually went ahead, they would have been even more irate.

Meanwhile, the sale of Leek, Leck and Robson had allowed Bowen to re-organise his squad. Following the purchase of Broadfoot, Graham Moore was signed for £15,000 from Manchester United.

The Cobblers' reputation as fierce competitors meant that many of their matches were likened to battlegrounds on muddy, churned up pitches. How appropriate then, that nearly forty years after the event, one of their most noble warriors should be found running a pub nine miles from Stamford Bridge in Yorkshire, scene of a major conflict in 1066.

Stamford Bridge? Sound familiar? Graham Moore had joined Chelsea from his first club Cardiff, and made his Cobblers debut against Tommy

Docherty's side on 27 December 1965, 900 or so years after the English King Harold notched a rare win on home soil.

The Cobblers' Christmas campaign in Division One that year also involved quickfire action, travel, and ultimate defeat. Chelsea ensured that Bowen's men began the year of England's World Cup triumph on the back foot, if not actually bottom of Division One. The Pensioners were 3-2 winners at the County Ground on the Monday afternoon in front of an official 23,275 (unofficially there were thousands more as a gate had been forced and many sampled the action for free).

In the return fixture, Chelsea won 1-0 with a late Barry Bridges header from Terry Venables' cross the next evening in London, during which Robson faced his former teammates.

Graham Moore was 24 years old, and after starting off as a centre-forward with Cardiff, became more of a deep-lying inside-forward or even a midfield player. Despite his experience at international level (he eventually won 21 caps) his experience of life in the big time was chequered. He courted a mixed reaction. He told me that after witnessing his Chelsea debut, the late Sam Leitch (best remembered as a 1970s football presenter on *Grandstand*) wrote in the *Daily Mirror* that he was the worst signing Chelsea had ever made.

Leitch was soon made to eat humble pie (making a personal retraction to Moore) after the Welshman struck two goals in a brave fight-back from 0-3 down against Tottenham. At this point a challenge from Ronnie Allen saw Moore stretchered off, and ten-man Chelsea lost 2-5.

Moore's debut for Manchester United on 9 November 1963 was also a lively affair. 'Wonderful,' he said. 'That side had so many good players.' It was the era of Gregg, Brennan, Foulkes, Crerand, Best, Law, Charlton, Sadler, Setters, Connolly and Stiles. How could you not revel in such company? United had thrashed Spurs, the double winners, two years earlier 4-1, with a hat-trick from Law and one by David Herd. Moore went on to play eighteen times that season, scoring his first goals in a red shirt in a 5-1 home drubbing of Burnley.

Yet the fact that Moore signed for Northampton in December 1965 was a clear indication his Old Trafford honeymoon did not last an eternity. A mixture of injuries and the quality of Matt Busby's side helped prompt his departure.

There was once a belief that most footballers gave up the game to run a pub, the theory being it enabled them to drink most of the profits. While there might be an occasional grain of truth in this, I am more interested in the modern shift towards eating out. The pub grub image is no longer a hairy green caterpillar which burrows into the salad. To my mind, not enough ex-pros run a pub. If the example of mine hosts Graham and Rita Moore is anything to go by, more should do so. It would have the added benefit of researching books an all-consuming occupation.

As a raw seventeen-year-old with Cardiff, Moore remembered meeting an appropriately named teammate Steve Gammon (who later became player-manager of Kettering) and Johnny Watkins for a pre-match meal of cottage pie, chips and peas. Football dieticians have moved the world forward substantially, although to my mind, chicken and beans has apparent limitations. Over to you Delia Smith ...

The home defeat by Chelsea also ended Foley's run of 88 consecutive league appearances, but he played in the return the next day, only to again be missing on New Year's Day 1966, when the side met Sheffield United. In the meantime, Leicester had done their bit for the Midlands cause by thumping Fulham 5-0 at Filbert Street, and the Cobblers earned a welcome point at Bramall Lane – goals by Lines and Martin earning a 2-2 draw.

Footage of Kenneth Wolstenholme presenting *Match of the Day* is the only Division One action I have ever watched, and I viewed the Sheffield United match in the living room of Carol Coe, widow of the Cobblers goalkeeper, who died of a brain tumour in 2001 at the age of sixty.

If Chesterfield is purported to be the spawning ground for English goalkeepers, perhaps Swansea does for the Welsh, as Coe was born within a mile of Gary Sprake and Jack Kelsey. He joined the Cobblers from Arsenal in 1960 and, though on the small side for a goalkeeper, was brave as a lion when it came to throwing himself at the feet of forwards. In total, he made 63 Cobblers appearances, coming back from the wilderness, or so it seemed, to replace Harvey during his period of poor form in Division One.

The Sheffield United contest was 'infamous' for Coe, on account of Mick Jones barging him aside when heading the first goal, which was hotly disputed. Coe waited until the second half for his revenge, when catching Jones in an 'off the ball incident' as Coe prepared to clear his lines. In later years, in watching the match video, he often remarked that 'Jones didn't trouble me again'.

The Cobblers recorded their first win of 1966 the following Saturday with a 2-1 win over Blackburn, the goals coming from Kiernan – from the edge of the penalty area – and Brown's header from Broadfoot's cross. Blackburn suffered in more ways than one this season. Just as the campaign was getting underway, the Lancashire town suffered a polio epidemic which led to the postponement of several matches and which, according to manager Jack Marshall, took an edge off their early season fitness. It almost classed his players as '20th Century lepers'.

Blackburn ended the season thirteen points behind the Cobblers. The Northampton argument has always been that had Rovers taken more points off others (remember they beat the Cobblers 6-1 at Ewood Park) it could have helped Bowen's men survive.

A three-day stop in Broadstairs acted as a prelude to the 1-1 draw at West Ham, where Northampton's first-half dominance was rewarded with a Brown goal from Broadfoot's pass, only for the Hammers to draw level when Coe lost a centre. Everitt was forced to touch the ball over the crossbar, conceding a penalty which Hurst converted. Everitt made three more conventional goal-line clearances in the second half as the Cobblers defended resolutely.

At the start of January, the President of FIFA, Stanley Rous, presided at the World Cup draw in London, and sixteen days later – in the most unlikely of scenarios – he was the special guest at the County Ground for the FA Cup third round 1-2 defeat by Nottingham Forest. He saw Brown head home a Lines cross for a Cobblers equaliser, the ball beating stand-in nineteen-year-old goalkeeper Jimmy Cargill, as Peter Grummitt had broken his thumb.

Imagine the following. It is July 1961 and Dave Bowen is acting as the modern quiz show host (for sake of argument, let's call it 4-3-2-1). Rous is the first contestant. Bowen: 'You're first question, Stanley. In four years time Northampton Town will be playing in Division One. True or false? There is loud laughter from the studio audience, but all the dignitary can do is shuffle uncomfortably in his seat. 'F-f-false … that must be false,' he finally blurts out. 'I'm sorry, Stanley, but it will be true!' The cameras pan away to Shirley Bassey singing 'Reach For The Stars (Climb Every Mountain)'.

Re-focusing on football, the following week Everton were the visitors. Harry Catterick's side were also carrying out a reconnaissance mission in the area, as they were also due to visit Bedford Town in another fortnight, in the fourth round of the FA Cup. Everton were Merseyside's sole rep-resentatives after holders Liverpool were beaten 1-2 at home by Chelsea.

At the County Ground, Everton were in front in the second minute, and although Gordon West saved well from Kiernan, and Brown headed onto the top of the bar, it was a disappointing day.

The Cobblers conceded six goals on four occasions during a season in which 100 were shipped in 45 league and cup matches. However, let's try and put this into perspective, for Bowen's men wouldn't have been the first to have shortcomings exposed at the highest level. Ask any Ipswich supporter. The 1961-62 Football League champions conceded 121 goals two seasons later, losing 1-10 at Fulham, 2-7 at home to Manchester United, and 1-9 at Stoke. It was those last two clubs who now handed out back-to-back 2-6 hammerings to the Cobblers on 5 and 12 February.

What have the following in common? Jeff Astle (West Brom), Willy Irvine (Burnley), George Jones (Blackburn Rovers), Bobby Charlton (Manchester United), John Ritchie (Stoke), and Steve Earle (Fulham). The answer is that they all scored hat-tricks against Northampton Town in Division One. And Charlton and Ritchie were about to strike ...

The Old Trafford trip mirrored Liverpool as an example of throwing modern day Christians to the lions. Graham Moore netted against his old club and Martin hit another in the second half, but the result was never in doubt.

Before the match, local journalists Mike Beesley and Fred Speakman, writing in the Northampton and Kettering newspapers, asked: 'Can the Cobblers succeed where Benfica failed?' The Red Devils had beaten their Portuguese opponents 1-0 in the European Cup quarter-final, first leg on the Wednesday. The fact that United went to Lisbon in March and won the second leg 5-1 should tell you everything.

Harry Walden was no slouch on the wing, but the memory persists of Charlton beating the Cobblers winger to a ball after giving him a twenty-yard start. 'They were a different dimension,' said one Cobblers player that day. Best, Law, Charlton and Stiles, they were all there. So too were future Northampton and Peterborough managers, Pat Crerand and Noel Cantwell.

Less excusable was a 2-6 drubbing at Stoke, although Foley missed the match with an ankle injury and Coe was virtually knocked out in the first minute as Stoke went in front. The hat-trick hero for the Potteries club was Ritchie, a former Kettering Town striker.

Perhaps fortunately for the Cobblers, it was also FA Cup fourth round day, 12 February 1966. Much attention was focused on Bedford Town's latest attempt at a giant-killing, this time against visitors Everton. Corby Town had also waved the local flag with distinction (winning 1-0 in a second round replay at Luton before crashing 0-6 at Plymouth in round three), but Bedford's reputation was enormous. They had drawn 2-2 at Arsenal in 1956 before losing the replay 1-2 at Goldington Road, and in 1964-65 had gone to the fourth round with a 2-1 win at Newcastle before bowing out 0-3 at home to Carlisle. Two goals by Everton's Derek Temple, though, punctured the dream in a five-minute spell before half-time. Fred Pickering added a third goal ten minutes from time, and Everton had carefully negotiated their banana skin *en route* to Wembley.

It needed the third round giant-killing exploits of those other Cup fighters, Walsall, to ensure the Cobblers were in action at all that day. The Division Three side had won 2-0 at Stoke in the third round, a result which allowed the Victoria Ground clash to be brought forward from Easter, avoiding two meetings between the clubs in two days.

Perhaps it should have stayed there, but from a positive standpoint, the effect of those back-to-back 2-6 horror shows at least allowed the club to re-focus and re-align for the final thirteen matches, from which the Cobblers would gather fifteen points.

Considering they didn't start this run in a relegation position, surely this would be enough to see them survive? Not a bit of it. Those thirteen matches were to prove unlucky.

CHAPTER EIGHT

SHORT, SWEET, AND NEVER TO BE FORGOTTEN

These boots are made for walkin',
And that's just what they'll do.
One of these days these boots are gonna
Walk all over you ...

Nancy Sinatra's hit was in the charts for fourteen weeks in 1966. It went to No 1 on 17 February, but during the week it was toppled, the Cobblers' own boots walked ... back to Division Two.

They should never have gone down. The structure of the club might never have been appropriate to Division One in 1965-66, but the efforts of its players never warranted relegation.

During the course of researching this book I spoke to 22 former players who wore claret and white during that campaign (23 if you count Bryan Harvey's green jersey). Almost unequivocally, to a man, they would say: 'We never deserved to go down.' So repetitive was it, that by the end the statement was almost boring and I had to disguise an uninterested glaze across my face. I even developed a unique shorthand squiggle for those immortal six words, which were usually followed by: 'We deserved at least one more season.'

It's difficult to remain stimulated once you've heard the same sentence 23 times. From about the fifteenth utterance, I suspect that my reply of: 'Oh really, how interesting!' – while hastily drawing a hand across my mouth to stifle a yawn – was lacking conviction. How embarrassing for all, as this had been my specialist subject for the last two and a half years, and to some degree a lifetime. After all, I had been brought up with this club. ('Oh my love, my life!')

What was being vocally drip-fed into me, was like some agonising form of Chinese water torture which still preyed on the minds of these players forty years later. And it was absolutely true. They *were* unlucky to go down (groan). The really unforgivable crime in most supporters' eyes was repeating the crime in Division Two the following season. Yet what would have happened if Northampton Town had preserved their top flight status for another twelve months? Unfortunately, we will never know the answer.

There's no doubt that they were unlucky in the end, although any team that waits fourteen matches before registering a first league win is asking for trouble. Bowen's men ended 1965-66 with 33 points, thirteen clear of Blackburn Rovers but two adrift of Fulham who also had a much better goal-average. The fact is that if you take the other thirteen other seasons between 1960-61 and 1973-74, a final tally of 33 would have been enough to survive in every case. (Chelsea and Luton were both relegated with 33 points in 1974-75, Leeds United had gone down with 34 in 1959-60, and Stoke City would suffer the same fate in 1976-77.) For the most part though, under the two-point system, 33 points would today be regarded as 'cool'.

Fifteen points from the final thirteen games represented a phenomenal run by a side which had spent most of its season in the relegation zone, but Fulham trumped that by getting twenty. Vic Buckingham's escapologists at Craven Cottage achieved nine wins, two draws and only two defeats. For heaven's sake, The Cottagers even won five away matches on the trot, at Aston Villa (5-2), West Ham (3-1), Leeds (1-0), the Cobblers (4-2) and Nottingham Forest (2-1). Even champions Liverpool only took eighteen points during that same final period. Fulham's form during the final third needed to be awesome, and it was.

Perhaps you could argue that with players such as Britain's first £100 a week footballer in Johnny Haynes, who made an incredible 594 league appearances for the Craven Cottage club between 1952-69 – as well as winning 56 full England caps – a youthful Bobby Robson, and World Cup hero George Cohen, whose nephew Ben would play rugby for Northampton more than three decades later, they should never have been in that position in the first place. It is of little consolation.

In February 1966, the fight was at its most intense. What beckoned was a nerve-racking finale. Could Northampton possibly survive?

One man who had a say in the fight was the Cobblers' No 10, Don Martin. Whenever this number shirt appeared on 'Spider's back during his career, it seemed that strange mystical forces tended to take over, which were otherwise redundant. This was especially true in Division One, when he netted seven goals in 28 league and cup appearances, yet none of those came during the eleven matches when he sported No 8 or No 9 (the latter just once, at home to Everton). In two spells with the Cobblers (he returned in 1975 after eight years at Blackburn), Martin made 252 league and cup appearances, scoring 82 goals in the process. He eventually wore every outfield shirt, bar the No 3, and is once rumoured to have taken over the goalkeeping jersey during his stay at Ewood Park. Martin's only double strike during the 1965-66 season came in the 3-1 win over Newcastle on 19 February, which raised optimism that Bowen's men could indeed pull off their escape.

In recent years the Don Martin Appreciation Society sprang to life in the Northamptonshire village of Mears Ashby and presented many fascinating (and a few less so) facts about their living Corby born 'legend', who first agreed to sign for the club while on a train returning to Northampton, after attending a trial at Arsenal.

As well as presenting a convincing argument that the Cobblers would have stayed up had he not missed the first eight matches of the season with the broken jaw sustained in a training accident, and been allowed to wear the No 10 shirt on a more regular basis (they won 40 per cent of their games when he did so), the Society shows that Martin is still out in front for firing the most League Cup goals in a Northampton shirt (eleven in eighteen games). It also points out that he also held the record for the club's record sale (£36,000) for eight years, after he joined Blackburn in 1968. That fee was surpassed by the £60,000 Liverpool paid Northampton for Phil Neal in 1974, so it is ironic to learn that Neal was once responsible for cleaning Martin's boots.

Few footballers can have been the subject of such an intensive study and hero worship from their local community. The Society also reveals that Martin shares his birthday (15 February) with such notables as the Emperor Nero, the Italian astronomer and physicist Galileo, the actress Jane Seymour and the West Indian cricketer Desmond Haynes. Key events in history which coincided with the date include the philosopher Socrates being sentenced to death (399), the Peace of Angleur (1313) and the first Teddy Bear to be introduced to America (1903).

Martin's first Cobblers goal had come at Newcastle in 1963 in a 3-2 win. Four days after his 22nd birthday he set the ball rolling by leaping high to head in Broadfoot's fifteenth minute free-kick to again set the Geordies on the back foot. Moore grabbed the second after Brown's blocked shot had fallen into his path, and Martin's second – a volley after a cross by Brown – helped secure the best home win of the season, despite Jim Iley's consolation with the last kick of the match.

With Fulham losing 3-4 at Spurs, it was good news all round, and when Martin continued his run of scoring in the eighth minute the following week – latching onto a Kiernan through ball to fire the ball past Ray Potter and put his side ahead at West Brom – there was further cause for optimism. However, two mistakes ensured Bowen's men would only secure a point that day. In the 22nd minute, Harvey failed to hold a blockbuster from John Kaye, and Clive Clark swept in the rebound, while early in the second half a fine Cobblers move almost carved out a winner in a mudbath made stickier by showers during a game which was only given the green light after two pitch inspections. Kurila broke up an Albion move and sent Moore clear, the striker drawing Stan Jones before slipping the ball to Brown, only for the striker to slice his shot wide.

Although the Cobblers had to defend in depth and a point was probably their deserved share, all this must have seemed more costly when the players returned to the dressing room to discover Fulham had beaten Liverpool 2-0. Liverpool had started the day ten points clear at the top but were beaten by two goals from Steve Earle in a match which saw Liverpool's Ian St John sent off for punching Mark Pearson. As far as the Cobblers were concerned, this was certainly an unexpected and disappointing blow.

Liverpool's closest pursuers included Leeds United, who had stayed in third place after a 1-1 draw at Sheffield United while Manchester United had swapped places with their 4-2 Old Trafford victims Burnley, moving into second spot in the process.

While the FA Cup had reached the fifth round stage (eventual winners Everton beating Coventry 3-0, and Sheffield Wednesday winning 2-1 at Huddersfield), Don Revie's Leeds were the Cobblers' next league opponents in the contest initially called off a week before Christmas. It was to prove a vintage day in the history of Northampton, with the star of the occasion undoubtedly George Hudson, once famously described as 'the best centre-forward never to play for England'.

Hudson became Bowen's last fling in the transfer market that season when he arrived at the County Ground for a £26,000 fee from Coventry City. His debut is still widely (and fondly) recalled by those of sufficient age, and a claret and white persuasion. The master craftsman with a 'Teddy Boy' style image, and film star looks scored goals for fun wherever he went, and he certainly went to some places. Blackburn Rovers, Accrington Stanley, Peterborough and Tranmere Rovers were the other clubs to benefit from his showman skills as he bagged 138 goals in 297 career league appearances.

No wonder Coventry's fans were irate at the sale of their top scorer that week. Some Sky Blues fans even made the (admittedly) shorter trip to Northampton, rather than see their own heroes despatched from the FA Cup at Goodison by way of protest.

In snapping up the services of Hudson, Bowen said: 'I feel we shall stay up now he has joined us. He may not have been getting goals just lately. But he is still Coventry's leading scorer with 17. My top scorer last year got 13 – and he was Robson, the outside-left.' Hudson's impact was immediate. In the eleventh minute he crossed for Lines to head a super goal from just inside the penalty area, and two minutes later he latched onto a Broadfoot pass before chipping the ball over Jackie Charlton, running on to crash home a fierce volley from sixteen yards. Although Mike O'Grady pulled a goal back for Leeds just two minutes later, the Cobblers held on for what remains the most notable league scalp in their 108 year history.

When I met up with George Hudson for what must rank as one of the more fascinating hours ever spent in a Tesco Coffee Shop (it was near Bury in October 2003), it would have been easy for him to acclaim the Leeds strike as the finest of his career. In fact, he placed it only second behind a Coventry goal he fired against Southampton at Highfield Road which at least summed up the type of flair of which he was capable. He recalled: 'A cross came from the right wing and I caught it on my right foot. I then chipped the ball over the defender Tony Knapp – which wasn't easy at 5ft 11in – ran round him and as the ball was dropping, headed it into the net.'

Attempting and scoring with chipped shots was a Hudson trade-mark, and one which he managed twice, even though his short and sweet Northampton stay lasted for just eighteen matches and six goals. After he netted with an audacious lob at Sheffield Wednesday he was challenged by Broadfoot, a man not averse to a bet, who wagered half a crown he couldn't repeat the trick. Hudson pulled off a similar stunt at Tottenham in April and collected his winnings.

Celebrations were in order after the Leeds win and it seems Hudson and Terry Branston spent much of it in the Pytchley Hotel in West Haddon, a natural stopping off point for both on the way back home to Rugby where, according to Branston, 'One of the local farmers made sure we didn't have to buy a drink all night.'

The pair travelled to matches together during Hudson's brief stop at Northampton. Hudson drove a Zodiac in the light blue colours of his previous club, and Branston's other fond recollection is of the car bumping along at 10mph in a high gear to the accompaniment of the words of Nancy Sinatra's *These Boots Are Made For Walkin'* while their heads almost bounced off the roof. If ever there was an appropriate theme song to an age, then surely this was it.

After such an inspiring success, it would have been easy for the visit of Nottingham Forest the following week to prove a let-down. That didn't happen, although the 3-3 draw offered less satisfaction, despite the fact John Kurila proved an unlikely goal-scoring hero.

Kurila played in the final sixteen games of the season after a brief four-match run from mid-September, and his injury-time leveller proved poetic justice as the Cobblers had been robbed by that 'handball' equaliser in the ninetieth minute at the City Ground, a contest which had marked Kurila's baptism in the top flight.

Such was the reputation of the man who made his Celtic debut in an Old Firm clash with Rangers, that he earned the nickname 'Crunch'. He had played in a Celtic reserve side which had won its league three years on the trot under Jock Stein, and which included the likes of Pat Crerand, Bertie Auld, John Clark, Billy McNeill, Bobby Murdoch and Tommy Gemmill. Later in his career he spent two seasons at Southend and Colchester, where he played a part in the famous 3-2 FA Cup victory over Leeds, which rocked the football nation. He also teamed up once more with Branston at Lincoln City.

A popular question and answer routine of the time went something like this: (Question) 'When did you know your leg was broken?' (Answer) 'When I saw John Kurila running towards me.' This was only half funny, and those in direct contact might say it barely qualified for a quarter. Kurila's approach embodied the Cobblers' approach and he admitted: 'We made sure we hit the man as well. For a lot of teams we were told that if you 'sort this one out' the game will be a lot easier. We had a lot of verbal from players such as Ian St John and Jeff Astle in Division One.'

This approach began on the training ground, and Kurila said: 'Practice games were very competitive. We changed the bibs around to get certain players in opposition. You had to be up for it.'

Against Forest, England centre-forward Joe Baker made his Forest debut after signing from Arsenal for £65,000, while future Northampton boss John Barnwell was also in the visitors' line-up. For the Cobblers, Branston was given a special cheer on the occasion of his 200th league appearance. Baker fired Forest in front early on, only for Martin to equalise with a back-header. Moore made it 2-1 early in the second half when he headed in a Lines cross. Ian Storey-Moore tied up the scoring at 2-2 on the hour and Baker appeared to have earned the visitors the points four minutes from time when he rammed home a loose ball after Harvey could only parry a Storey-Moore drive. But in the dying seconds, the Cobblers won a corner and, after two efforts were blocked, Kurila's shot was deflected off a defender and into the roof of the net.

Cobblers manager Bowen had developed an astute sense of business which had clearly brought rewards, and he deserved backing up to the hilt. However, as any speculator will tell you, not every coup you attempt comes off, and there's no doubt that the signing of winger Broadfoot fell into that category.

It's ironic that in the week the Cobblers prepared to travel to Sheffield Wednesday, Bury wing-half and captain Colin Bell should finally move to Manchester City for £45,000. Bell had been one of the rising stars Bowen had endeavoured to sign, at one point lining up Carr and Best as makeweights as part of a deal to go in the opposite direction. But in the same way that Bowen resisted offers from high-profile clubs such as Arsenal and Everton for players such as Kiernan and Lines, so he was never able to pull off the Bell deal.

It was nobody's fault that the Broadfoot swoop was not a success, although the player did not fit naturally into the tactical work ethic employed at Northampton. This meant Bowen was probably years ahead of his time as a coach in achieving what he did. He once tried to sum up the turbulence of the roller coaster years by offering the words: 'By the time we reached Division One, some of the players were like dry flannels. I couldn't wring any more out of them.' When the cash signings did come along – in the form of Broadfoot, Moore and Hudson – it was almost too late.

Broadfoot was fast, devilishly fast. Full-back Mike Everitt was no slouch either, and there's a story that Broadfoot once challenged him to a race along the length of the County Ground pitch. Everitt was given an eighteen-yard start, from the edge of one penalty area, but Broadfoot still beat him.

The winger 'Pretty Joey', as he was labelled by some, had clearly been a talent for Millwall and Ipswich. Even in the 1-10 hiding which Ipswich endured at Fulham on Boxing Day 1963, Broadfoot liked to recall the quote from Bobby Robson: 'The best player on the pitch was wearing an Ipswich shirt and that was Joe Broadfoot.'

The problem was (and here lay the rub for Ipswich) that Broadfoot had never been asked to chase back under Ipswich boss Jackie Milburn, and Bowen's game was built around an entirely different philosophy. Broadfoot said: 'Northampton looked after me financially. I signed for the club after meeting Dave Bowen and Ray Osborne in a hotel in the town centre and they instantly slapped £200 on the table and said: "Thanks for coming." I was made a payment of £2,500 just for agreeing to sign.' He added: 'I admit Northampton didn't get the best of me but it wasn't something I wanted to happen. It just didn't work out.'

Dressing-room harmony was another area not helped by Broadfoot's presence in the side, a fact which became apparent to me in the summer of 2004 when I asked the player to sign an autograph across his photograph in a pictorial Northampton Town history. Broadfoot happily complied with the request, only to then notice that a picture on the facing page was an old teammate with whom he had once had (in polite language) a 'contretemps'. He looked up and said: 'Do you realise that every time those pages are slammed shut it's as though I get head-butted again.'

Bowen's patience with Broadfoot almost ran out at Hillsborough, where in a dressing-room inquest, the player's lack of heart was brought into question. When turned upon, it brought from the player the memorable quote: 'I can't help it ... a leopard can't change its spots.'

Even following the disappointing 1-3 defeat at Sheffield Wednesday, Bowen didn't entirely scrub Broadfoot out of the equation. He was asked to report for duty for the Fulham game in April, only for his E-Type Jaguar to break down on the motorway near Luton. To say that this incident severed any final connection would be to enter the realms of understatement. The final irony in the Broadfoot v Northampton story came in January the following season, when the club were struggling in Division Two. Broadfoot arrived back at the County Ground with Millwall and scored a header from a free-kick in a 2-1 victory. Talk about rubbing it in.

The Owls' first win at Hillsborough in 1966 also marked the Cobblers debut of 22-year-old John Mackin, who came on as an early substitute for the injured Barry Lines. When Theo Foley was also injured, Mackin switched from attack to defence – an early pointer to the versatility of the Corby youngster, who would serve the club so well during the next difficult three years, before briefly joining Lincoln City en route to three years at York City.

There could be few complaints about the ending of the four-match unbeaten run, as Wednesday struck the woodwork four times. It was a day when the Division One highlight saw Tony Hateley score four times as Aston Villa came from 1-5 down to draw 5-5 at Tottenham in the highest scoring match in the division that season. Villa's other scorer was Alan Deakin, brother of ex-Cobbler Mike, while former Northampton skipper Laurie Brown, Alan Gilzean, Jim Robertson, Jimmy Greaves and Frank Saul scored for Spurs.

Skipper Foley passed a late fitness test to return at home to Leicester the following Saturday evening, but this proved a mistake. He lasted only six minutes and the knee injury kept him out for the duration of the campaign when his presence was sorely missed.

Foley's influence on the side was immeasurable, coupling his competitive edge and terrier-like tackling with an ability to keep chattering. They were key factors in his role as a captain, and his replacement, Moore, proved a somewhat reluctant skipper, passing on the task to Branston the following season, when Foley was out until January.

Theo summed up the time when, in the 1964-65 souvenir promotion programme, he said: 'No stars – but in fact, just what are stars anyway? We all pull together and, most important, we are well led by a man this town should never forget, Dave Bowen.'

Foley went to Charlton at the end of 1966-67 (in fact his last Cobblers match was at The Valley). His considerable management career ultimately took him to the top, as assistant to George Graham for Arsenal's 1988-89 Division One title-winning season (the pair had also won promotion together with Millwall in 1984-85). It speaks volumes that he gave all that up to return to manage a 'down on their luck' Northampton in 1990, describing it as 'the job I always wanted'.

Away from the football field, Foley and Bowen sowed business seeds in the town. When the chip and pie shop 'Foley's Bake-N-Take' opened on Kingsthorpe shopping front at the height of the Cobblers' success, Foley invited the singer Ruby Murray – wife of his friend Bernie Burgess – to mark the occasion. Murray had enjoyed acclaim as a singer in the 1950s with a No 1 hit *Softly Softly* and other successes such as *Heartbeat, If Anyone Finds This I Love You* and *Evermore*, and the Foleys were regular visitors to the couple's home at Wootton. When Foley and his wife Sheila moved to London, Murray performed a show at Charlton's club. Even the singer's untimely death did not sever the long-term friendship with Burgess, who began life working for the New Theatre in Abington Street and now lives in Spain.

Foley's typical 'hands on' approach saw him helping out in the shop on occasions, with his other business associate, Tony Hepworth, who ran the Kinsons café in Northampton's town centre St Giles Street for many years. Foley said: 'Even now I remember buying in the Fleur de Lys pies from Coventry and burning my hands on the pastry flakes.'

Meanwhile, Bowen followed the example of his parents, Martha and Bryn, in the way of business acumen. You might even say he had fingers in a number of pies. When the Bowen family severed their connection with the Roadmender Club, they ran the Plumbers Arms pub, a stone's throw away on Sheep Street. Although that closed down and became a gun shop, plans were afoot for it to become a pub once more, just as this book was approaching publication. Couple that with the fact that Northampton Town were preparing their Division One fortieth anniversary season with a tour of Austria, and you realise that everything comes around eventually. Maybe even promotion …

Martha Bowen took on the Newlands sweet shop in the town centre, where the name 'Bowen' appeared for many years, alongside that of 'Collins' on the sports shop in Gold Street. Add to that the Emporium

Café in the Arcade next to the Market Square, the grocer's shop Gandy's on the (Market) Harborough Road, and Bowen's tentative latter-day dabbling in the bookmaker business, and you begin to understand that a lifetime's habit of family wheeler-dealing was only ever going to gently slow down, rather than disappear altogether.

Without Foley, the Cobblers drew a match with Leicester they might easily have won. Indeed, if there are suggestions of a conspiracy theory surrounding some of Fulham's late season results against the Division One elite, there's also a school of thought that believed Leicester tried to 'throw' this one for the benefit of Northampton. Certainly, they had no reason to be as committed as Bowen's men, starting the game in ninth place in the league table.

Snow had fallen in the town the day before this Saturday evening kick-off, a switch made due to the Grand National in the afternoon. This allowed the club's directors to join their Leicester counterparts for a pre-match meal at the Sywell Airport Hotel, but the evening's events would have digested more easily had the necessary two points been served up as a very acceptable nightcap.

Gordon Banks had just returned from injury when the sides had first met in Division One, and the great England goalkeeper was between the posts for this one. A youthful Jacqui Tyson, who many years later would marry a future Northampton Town chairman in Barry Stonhill, was a programme seller at the time and recalled: 'I sold Gordon Banks a programme that night. The next person I saw was my English teacher Mr Hill who made me write an essay about the Cobblers the following week.'

Banks was quickly beaten by Hudson in the return game, only for Mike Stringfellow to equalise. Before half-time, Walden – playing his first match since November – made a run and centre, allowing Moore to lob the ball over Banks for a 2-1 lead. It should have been game, set and match to the Cobblers, but Harvey's slip, which allowed Jackie Sinclair's long-range shot to beat him, and a preposterous series of near misses at the other end, meant it wasn't to be.

Twice in Division One the Cobblers came from behind to win. Both occasions cropped up in the final seven matches. The first was in front of the smallest league crowd of the season at Villa Park, a match which started in a snowstorm and ended in a blizzard. Perhaps the Cobblers wore their white shirts through some act of camouflage? Willie Hamilton put the home side ahead after Tony Hateley had pulled a ball back from the by-line but within three minutes of the turnaround young goalkeeper John Gavan failed to hold a long range free-kick by Mackin under pressure from Hudson, and the Cobblers were gifted an equaliser.

Villa had been the more dominant side in the first half, and still had enough chances to win it, although Hudson twice hit the bar with solo efforts at the other end. The winner arrived when Lines broke away to give Moore all the time in the world to score. Suddenly, anything seemed possible. In the *Chronicle & Echo*, Michael Beesley was in an upbeat mood with the Cobblers on target for what they believed would be their 'safety' target of 33 points. Oh, if only!

In the Home Internationals, England clinched the series with a 4-3 win over Scotland at Hampden Park, with goals by Geoff Hurst (two), Bobby Charlton and Roger Hunt. Northampton fans though, were more concerned with the Division One dogfight. Although Blackburn stayed adrift, Fulham's 2-1 win over West Brom kept them just two points behind with two games in hand, although as many as eight clubs were within four points ahead of Bowen's men.

Easter Saturday brought quagmire conditions, unrelenting rain and leaders Liverpool to the County Ground. It didn't, though, bring Roger Hunt, who had been injured at Hampden Park. Bill Shankly's men were on course for their seventh championship and there was a noticeable tension in the Hotel End crowd. A 0-0 draw was creditable for the Cobblers and probably good enough for Liverpool, although nearest rivals Burnley defeated Sunderland 1-0. The day was also remarkable for Manchester United suffering their first defeat in 41 games at Old Trafford: they were beaten 1-2 by Leicester.

Northampton's 1-0 defeat of Stoke three days later, earned with a Martin strike early in the second half, should have given them a healthy cushion from the relegation zone. Imagine then, the sense of disbelief and horror when news filtered through that Fulham had triumphed 1-0 at Leeds with a goal by Mark Pearson.

Fulham were at it again four days later with a 4-2 win over Sheffield Wednesday. They then reverted back to old bad habits on the following Monday with a 0-4 home defeat by Leicester. The match was watched by the entire Cobblers squad, as their Midlands neighbours once again did their bit in trying to save on future travel expenses.

Cottagers manager Vic Buckingham missed seeing his side's game with the Owls, preferring instead to carry out a spying mission himself on the Cobblers in their 1-1 draw with Tottenham at White Hart Lane. In fact, Bowen and Buckingham bumped into one another in a corridor after the game, which had seen Hudson chip the Cobblers into a first-half lead. That was wiped out by Jimmy Greaves' penalty twelve minutes from time, after Everitt had been forced to handle a fierce shot by Laurie Brown on the goal-line.

'Spying on us again Vic?' asked Bowen with a grin, to which the former Tottenham wing-half quipped: 'I've just come to do a spot of training.' The light-hearted banter thinly masked the 'winner takes all' significance of the Fulham game, which was looming large at the County Ground the following Saturday. It was a contest neither side could afford to lose.

There was a further significant knock on to the Fulham game from the spirited point the Cobblers had earned at Tottenham, since the man Greaves beat from the spot was Mackin and not Harvey. The Cobblers goalkeeper had finally been forced from the field after a third visit from trainer Joe Payne, having taken a nasty kick on the spine diving at the feet of Alan Mullery at the start of the second half.

It meant a battle for fitness which would not be decided until the morning of the most critical game in the Cobblers' history. Like the final outcome, it was a battle which was lost in front of the biggest gathering ever to assemble for a football match at the County Ground. A crowd of 24,523 witnessed the Cobblers' 2-4 defeat that day.

Apart from the inclusion of Norman Coe for Harvey, there were no fresh injury worries. In fact, the Cobblers did not have to make an outfield change for their final seven matches, although Moore and Martin juggled the No 8 and No 10 shirts. At 3pm on 23 April, 1965 the bottom six placings in Division One were as follows:

	P	W	D	L	F	A	Pts
17 Sunderland	39	13	7	19	47	69	33
18 Aston Villa	38	13	6	19	63	72	32
19 Sheff Wed	36	12	7	17	50	58	31
20 COBBLERS	39	9	13	17	51	84	31
21 Fulham	38	12	5	21	59	80	29
22 Blackburn	36	7	4	25	51	77	18

It was also FA Cup semi-finals day. Sheffield Wednesday defeated Chelsea 2-0 at Villa Park, while Everton beat Manchester United 1-0 with a Colin Harvey goal. In the league, Sunderland's 1-1 draw at Arsenal was another result the Cobblers could have done without.

Fulham welcomed back Johnny Haynes after three matches missing with a calf-muscle injury, and they also included their recent striker signing Alan Clarke, who had proved a prolific marksman with his first league club, Walsall.

The Cobblers, though, were quickest out of the traps. In the opening minutes Moore's header came back off the crossbar. Walden's follow-up was cleared off the line by defender Brian Nichols as he tumbled back into his goal. Far from being disheartened, Northampton then raced into a thirteenth-minute lead. The Fulham defence retreated in the face of Kiernan's fifty-yard run, and when Northern Ireland goalkeeper John McClelland could only parry his shot, Hudson followed up.

Fulham equalised six minutes later when Bobby Robson fired inside the right-hand post after collecting a return pass from Mark Pearson, but Kiernan made it 2-1 when Robson failed to head Walden's cross to safety and the Cobblers' schemer netted with a crisp shot.

In simple goalscoring terms, it was then a case of 'enter Steve Earle', but before the young Fulham winger equalised in the 64th minute there came two defining moments. Had either of two decisions gone the Cobblers way, a 3-1 lead would have been established and much might have changed.

Before the break Mackin's flighted free-kick dropped over McClelland and inside the post. Referee Jack Taylor though, disallowed the effort, apparently for a foul on the goalkeeper. Far more famously, the future World Cup final official ruled out Hudson's second-half shot. The ball – in the eyes of many of those present – had been spooned back from behind the line by McClelland, after the keeper had parried it up in the air. Taylor, looking for guidance from his linesman, saw the official flat on his back by the corner flag, caught out by the speed of events. In dismissing Kiernan's protest with the words: 'Sorry Joe, I didn't see it, I can't give it,' Taylor unwittingly turned the tide of events.

Earle equalised when he turned in Cohen's right-wing cross, and although both sides stretched their sinews in the search for a winner, it was Fulham who struck twice with time almost up to clinch their eighth win in ten matches. Graham Leggat's cross was headed in by Earle, whereupon the entire Northampton team, bar Coe, lined up on the halfway line for the restart This desperate action, while laudable in its intent, only served to allow Earle to scamper clear onto a Robson pass, round Coe, and hammer in the day's final nail.

Earle's reaction was not surprising. 'I felt good when I got our second equalising goal, but when I scored those two in two minutes I really felt ten feet tall.' Meanwhile, the reaction of England legend Haynes revealed just how close Fulham had come to disaster. 'If Northampton had played in the second half as they did in the first, I think they must have won. I was certainly worried at half-time, but they went back on defence and gave us all the room in the world.'

In the Cobblers camp, the hardest of grown men was seen to break down and weep. Perhaps most poignant of all was Bowen's reaction: 'We are, maybe, not dead. But there's not much life left now.' The defeat left the Cobblers needing plenty of other results to go their way.

At least they aided their cause by beating Sunderland 2-1 two days later, coming from behind with goals by Everitt and Hudson, after Neil Martin had posted a 28th-minute lead for the visitors. Everitt's 22-yard rocket, with just 21 minutes left, eased some tension and produced another notable landmark for a player who had now played, and scored for the club (like Lines) in all four divisions. 'Pinky', as he was known to teammates, was another classic example of what could achieved with a little willpower. Converted to left-back, he played 32 times in Division One with most of his games in that position. Yet he wasn't even a natural left-footed player. Later Everitt would play for Plymouth and Brighton before entering the hazardous world of management with Brentford, while later profiting from regular coaching terms in Dubai.

Ironically, the Sunderland win meant the Cobblers briefly occupied the highest position they had held all season – eighteenth. The writing though, still screamed out loudly in big, bold letters from the wall. Before the final journey to Blackpool, on 30 April, wins for Sheffield Wednesday (2-0 over Aston Villa) and Fulham (2-1 at Nottingham Forest) had seen Northampton drop to twentieth, one place above the safety line. Villa had two extra games to play, trailed by just a point, and enjoyed a far superior goal-average.

It needed a Cobblers victory at Bloomfield Road, and then a huge amount of hope. Fantasy believers, or simply those inspired by epics on the big screen, might have taken heart from the fact that Bowen and the side spent part of the night on Friday, 29 April watching the *Sound Of Music* in a Blackpool cinema.

Unlike the von Trappe family, though, the Cobblers own escape path had been effectively sealed up. There was to be no belated climb to freedom. Blackpool needed a point themselves to be mathematically sure of surviving and after a goalless first half, played in glorious sunshine, it was Bowen's men who wilted in the heat as goals by winger Les Lea, Ian Moir and an Alan Ball penalty – after Branston had upended Ray Charnley – shattered the dream. When the final whistle blew and news came through that Aston Villa had beaten Arsenal 3-0 at Villa Park, everyone knew that the game was up. The dream ride had come to an end.

Chapter Nine

See You at the Far Post

No club has emulated the Cobblers' remarkable nine-year journey, ending back where it started, though several have tried. Its speed was unrelenting. If the Division One relegation of 1965-66 deserves to be filed among lists of heroic failures, surely the drop from Division Two a season later is indexed in the club history under 'D' for Disaster. There was a brief pause in Division Three (eighteenth place in 1967-68), before another relegation in 1968-69.

After that final-day drama at Blackpool, season 1965-66 concluded with a goal by Harry Walden, which clinched a Northants Senior Cup success at rivals Peterborough. There followed a ten-day trip to Germany, although Bowen and Graham Moore toured with the Welsh party to South America.

In Germany, the Cobblers were beaten 0-3 by Hanover, but defeated Ruesselsheim 3-1 and FSV Eintracht Trier 2-1. It lightened the mood, for there was much to be thankful for. Surely it was not inconceivable that the club could bounce straight back?

For one thing, the reserves had enjoyed a great season in Division One of the Football Combination, finishing fourth behind champions Tottenham, Arsenal and Peterborough, which suggested the club was blessed with a degree of strength in depth. Once Combination matches had been switched to Tuesday evenings, rarely did attendances drop below 3,000. The biggest of them saw 6,553 attend the 1-1 draw with Arsenal on 8 February, but Roly Mills' side was generally a free-scoring outfit. Its finest exponent was Billy Best, who cracked 27 goals as he tried to make a case for first-team football.

The biggest home victories saw Ipswich and Cardiff hammered 6-0, Chelsea on the end of a 5-0 hiding, while both Spurs and Nottingham Forest left the County Ground on the back of 4-1 defeats.

Life back in Division Two though, was to prove a dreadful anticlimax. Twenty-four of the 42 league matches were lost and not even the return of Frank Large at Christmas could stop the rot, although he scored eight goals in 21 games to be second top scorer behind Don Martin, who again struck thirteen in the league, just as he had in 1964-65. This time though, he also hit six League Cup goals.

The highlights, and there were precious few, included a fourth round 8-0 League Cup replay win at home to Brighton in November, in which

Martin bagged four, Moore two, with a Best strike and an own-goal completing the tally. West Brom proved too hot in the next round when they won 3-1 at the County Ground.

Dave Bowen stepped down from the manager's hot seat during the 1967-68 campaign, shortly after the arrival of former England and Wolves wing-half Ron Flowers as player-coach, with Tony Marchi taking charge of team affairs. Flowers replaced Marchi the following season but that did nothing to arrest the dramatic slide.

If one match ever summed up a club's decade it was surely, in the Cobblers case, a home game with Shrewsbury Town on 8 April, 1969. The club were still comfortably clear of the relegation zone and survival appeared more or less guaranteed when they led 3-0 at half-time, thanks to goals from Frank Rankmore, John Roberts and a youthful Phil Neal. Somehow though, they contrived to turn this score into a 3-4 defeat, with Flowers responsible for one of two own-goals. Four defeats and a draw followed in the final five matches, and when Gillingham secured the point they needed on the final day of the season – with a 1-1 draw against that same Shrewsbury side – Northampton Town had once more hit rock bottom.

Of the 25 players who wore a Northampton Town shirt during 1965-66, Charlie Livesey and Norman Coe had moved on to 'a better place' at the time this book was published. Ten others – Billy Best, Graham Carr, Brian Etheridge, Bryan Harvey, Joe Kiernan, John Kurila, Ken Leek, John Mackin, Don Martin and Harry Walden – are still settled in Northamptonshire, while Terry Branston (Rugby) and Barry Lines (Bletchley) are within a comfortable half an hour drive, having never moved from their home town.

Strikers Jim Hall and Bobby Brown are east and western poles apart, craning their necks for a sea view, both within a couple of miles of Great Yarmouth and Haverfordwest respectively, the latter involved with the family-run Rising Sun pub, which also offers Bed & Breakfast to football supporters planning yet another 'great escape'.

The pub landlord business also attracted Graham Moore in North Yorkshire, while a trip to London unearths Theo Foley and Joe Broadfoot, who still attends 'old boy' reunions at Ipswich and Millwall. Vic Cockcroft now takes a back seat from finance near Coventry, George Hudson enjoys a game of bowls in Bury, while Derek Leck has now retired from the bakery trade, just a ten-minute drive from the sea front at Brighton.

Tommy Robson works in the newspaper business in Peterborough, while offering his thoughts on football as an expert analyst for local radio, while Bobby Hunt is back home in Colchester and Mike Everitt is domiciled on the Isle of Man. He never minded travelling (after all, he elected to sign for Plymouth and spent years coaching in Dubaï) and in recent years has fitted in the odd game of golf with Harvey (a pursuit much loved by skipper Foley) while also looking in on mine host Moore at his hostelry at Burythorpe ...

Much of the 'beauty' of the Cobblers' epic journey lies in the fact that the trip was neatly packaged within the 1960s. Nine seasons, made up of three promotions, three relegations and only three spent simply pausing for a breather.

There was little hint, following the 1-2 home defeat by Watford on 28 December 1959, when the curtain fell on the 1950s, that the '60s would be anything unusual or different. Idly skip forward to a goalless draw at Lincoln on 27 December 1969 and you find Northampton Town languishing three-quarters of the way down Division Four, peacefully it seems, minding their own business. Bowen's men could easily have spent the last ten years there, dust and cobwebs forming on and around the old wooden main (and only!) permanent stand.

In fact, while the Cobblers were preparing for an FA Cup-tie at Brentwood *en route* to that infamous fifth round 2-8 drubbing by Manchester United on 7 February 1970 – the day George Best scored six goals – Swansea City were starting a journey which would see them come closest to matching those roller-coaster years.

After finishing third in Division Four that season, the Swans' more sedate progress saw them repeat that position in Division Three nine years later before another third in Division Two in 1980-81. Under John Toshack they achieved a best ever league placing of sixth in Division One in 1981-82. Relegated the following season, they were back in Division Four in 1986. A sixteen-year circle is truly a 'grand tour', while not in the Northampton class for clinical efficiency.

Carlisle supporters rotate around a 22-year cycle. The Cumbrians' 1974-75 season in Division One is fondly recalled by their supporters, ten years after they were runners-up to Gillingham in Division Four in 1964-65. In 1987 they returned to the basement. You could argue that their 2004 relegation to the Conference took the ride a step further.

Notts County rose from Division Four as champions in 1969-70, played in Division One between 1981-84, before slipping back down to the basement again in 1997. This represented a mere 27-year cycle. Oxford United were elected to the league in 1962 and after winning promotion in 1964-65 reached the glorified heights of Division One in 1985, winning the Milk Cup the following year. They returned to football's bottom rung in 2001 after a long-winded grind of some 36 years.

What of Wimbledon, I hear you cry? Their story has truly been a remarkable one. Elevated to league status in 1977, the seasons 1987-2000 were spent in the First Division or the Premiership, so this is truly the stuff of *Boys' Own*. Their new life in the skin of MK Dons though, assuredly breaks the chain.

Leyton Orient finished bottom of Division One in 1962-63, having been members of Division Three (South) as late as 1956. They returned to Division Four in 1985, while Wolves' sorry flirtation with Division Four life between 1986-88 brought back only fleeting memories of their less than heady Division Three (North) season in 1923-24. Back in the Premiership for 2003-04, they are not obvious candidates to adopt the slide-rule theory again, although their stay in the top flight was brief.

Dave Bowen's association with Northampton Town Football Club continued to the day he died on 25 September 1995, at which point he was still the club president. When he acknowledged that his magic of inspiring sides to achieve great feats had dimmed – handing over team affairs to Tony Marchi in 1967 – he continued to actively serve the club for many years as general manager, secretary and scout.

Bowen and his wife Audrey had three children. Lynn, the eldest, was born on 14 September 1954, just eight days before her father won his first Welsh cap against Yugoslavia, a match which was lost 1-3. Sons Barry and Keith were both born in Northampton, and played football to a decent level, although it was Keith who pursued a professional career with Northampton, Brentford and Colchester. While never glitzing the national or international path on which his father trod, he does at least have the distinction of marrying a girl named Beckham.

Such was Dave Bowen's profile in the 1960s, there remains no doubt he could have managed at a more fashionable club at home or abroad (he even visited Greece to discuss taking on the Olympiakos job). Somehow though, he was always happiest around a club he knew, although home life often took a back seat, in favour of relentless scouting missions. Even a civic reception at Northampton Town Hall to mark promotion to Division One wasn't considered the highest priority ... Bowen was late arriving at the bean feast after a scouting trip to Shrewsbury.

The key to the success of any football manager is his 'network', and Bowen's contacts book was weighty. There was though, one contact he didn't anticipate. Arriving at the British Embassy in Moscow in May 1965 prior to a Welsh World Cup qualifier with the Soviet Union (which was lost 1-2), the Welsh national team boss was greeted by his next door neighbour, Peter Johnson, who lived at 17 Thornby Drive. Audrey Bowen recalled: 'Dave was totally shocked. He didn't have any idea at the time that our neighbour in Kingsthorpe worked in the diplomatic service.'

In later years I can still recall one of Bowen's favourite clichés: 'The only certainty is the uncertainty.' Whether inspired by football, horse racing (remember he once owned a bookmakers) or the man from No 17, I will never know. His other favourite phrase was to holler down the street: 'See you at the far post,' (I like to imagine the word 'boyo' in a rich Welsh lilt as a postscript, although I suspect he never said that himself) and my respected friend and journalist John Morris insists these were the last words Bowen ever spoke to him.

Morris was the former *Chronicle & Echo* reporter who returned to the town after a lengthy stint on the nationals to buy the freelance sports agency from Fred Speakman, himself something of a legend. Speakman was a press-box doyen during five decades of covering sport from the County Ground. A a quintessential 'character', he is worthy of more than simply passing reference during a memorable age.

When uttered down a phone-line to copytakers in London, the opening shot: 'Speakman, Northampton,' earned instant respect, for the recipient knew (if at all experienced) that what was to follow, was good, accurate stuff. Yet the archetypal bachelor was renowned in press-boxes for stuffing sandwiches in the pockets of an old overcoat and heating up meat over the electric fire in his Christchurch Road flat. In newspaper circles, Speakman was secretary of the Northampton Press Ball and memorably arrived for the function one year dressed in his dinner jacket and wellies. If Northampton Town were ever regarded as a 'rag, tag and bobtail' outfit by the elite during their season in the sun, at least they were consistent to the core.

Working in the modest surroundings in which he did, there would have been no sense in Bowen doing more than simply tackling the next job on the list, always with the minimum of fuss. Doubtless then, he would have concurred with the club's record goalscorer Jack English, who was once asked to explain his lack of elation when hitting the target (he even used to discourage teammates). English's riposte was to say: 'As a footballer it was part of my job to score goals. If I had been a plumber it would have been part of my job to fit taps, and I would not have wanted other plumbers rushing up and congratulating me every time I fitted a tap correctly!'

Perhaps he was inspired by the incident of Mike Deakin fixing the toilet at Hartlepool, who knows? Yet the secret of those heady days at the top for everyone was pulling together, weaving in a fabric of loyalty throughout the club and into a community who were happy to embrace the club characters and their success. The money wasn't great, as more than one of the 'grass root' Northampton '60s players intimated during the course of researching this book. 'We were on £25 a week if we weren't in the first team, but we could make that up to £35 by getting there,' one player told me. 'The difference to what happens today is that we were on the same sort of money as the men in the factory who we would play skittles with in the pub on a Thursday night.'

On the journey to Division One, Bowen's skill as a tactician, psychoanalyst and manipulator ensured Northampton Town were one step ahead of the game. In Division One, the money counted, although nowhere nearly as much as it counts today.

Interviewed by a national newspaper just weeks before the golden age was to come to an end, the Cobblers' own patron saint appeared to open his heart to the nation ... 'I'm very ambitious,' Bowen explained. 'There's an awful lot I'd love to do here, but ...' at this point he shrugged his shoulders, before signing off: 'I wish I had Chelsea's money.'

And he said that in 1966, not four decades later!

GUIDE TO SEASONAL SUMMARIES

Col 1: Match number (for league fixtures); Round (for cup-ties).
e.g. 4R means 'Fourth round replay.'

Col 2: Date of the fixture and whether Home (H), Away (A), or Neutral (N).

Col 3: Opposition.

Col 4: Attendances. Home gates appear in roman; Away gates in *italics*.
Figures in **bold** indicate the largest and smallest gates, at home and away.
Average home and away attendances appear after the final league match.

Col 5: Respective league positions of Cobblers and opponents after the game.
Cobblers' position appears on the top line in roman.
Their opponents' position appears on the second line in *italics*.
For cup-ties, the division and position of opponents is provided.
e.g. 2:12 means the opposition are twelfth in Division 2.

Col 6: The top line shows the result: W(in), D(raw), or L(ose).
The second line shows Cobblers' cumulative points total.

Col 7: The match score, Cobblers' given first.
Scores in **bold** show Cobblers' biggest league win and heaviest defeat.

Col 8: The half-time score, Cobblers' given first.

Col 9: The top line shows Cobblers' scorers and times of goals in roman.
The second line shows opponents' scorers and times of goals in *italics*.
A 'p' after the time of a goal denotes a penalty; 'og' an own-goal.
The third line gives the name of the match referee.

Team line-ups: Cobblers' line-ups appear on top line, irrespective of whether
they are home or away. Opposition teams are on the second line in *italics*.
Players of either side who are sent off are marked !
Cobblers' players making their league debuts are displayed in **bold**.

No	Date		Att Pos	Pt	F-A	H-T	Scorers, Times, and Referees	1	2	3	4	5	6	7	8	9	10	11
1	24/8	A MIDDLESBROUGH	27,122 20 2	L 0	0-1	0-0	Horsfield 90 / Ref: J Carr	Harvey	Foley	Everitt	Leck	Branston	Kiernan	**Walden**	Hunt	**Livesey**	Martin	Lines
								Connachan	*Gates*	*Jones*	*Townsend*	*Nurse*	*Orritt*	*Kaye*	*Gibson*	*Horsfield*	*Irvine*	*Braithwaite*

Middlesbrough had won 3-0 at Southampton on Saturday, with the Cobblers idle. Livesey and Walden make debuts, but history is repeated. Bowen's men had lost 1-0 at Ayresome Park to an 87th-minute goal in April, and Horsfield's winner here arrives 50 seconds into injury-time.

No	Date		Att Pos	Pt	F-A	H-T	Scorers, Times, and Referees	1	2	3	4	5	6	7	8	9	10	11
2	29/8	A MANCHESTER C	20,935 12 13	W 2	2-0	1-0	Foley 39p, Hunt 61 / Ref: S Stookes	Harvey	Foley	Everitt	Leck	Branston	Kiernan	Walden	Hunt	Livesey	Martin	Lines
								Dowd	*Bacuzzi*	*Kennedy*	*Gray*	*Cheetham*	*Oakes*	*Pardoe*	*Stobart*	*Murray*	*Kevan*	*Connor*

George Poyser's City had thrashed Leyton Orient 6-0 three days earlier but the Cobblers secure their first points of the season thanks to a first-half penalty, awarded after Martin is charged in the back, and a 20-yard drive by Hunt who latched onto Walden's through ball before scoring.

No	Date		Att Pos	Pt	F-A	H-T	Scorers, Times, and Referees	1	2	3	4	5	6	7	8	9	10	11
3	1/9	H MIDDLESBROUGH	17,028 12 3	D 3	1-1	0-1	Martin 65 / Horsfield 19 / Ref: G Davis	Harvey	Foley	Everitt	Leck	Branston	Kiernan	Walden	Hunt	Livesey	Martin	Lines
								Connachan	*Gates*	*Jones*	*Townsend*	*Nurse*	*Orritt*	*Kaye*	*Gibson*	*Horsfield*	*Irvine*	*Braithwaite*

Raich Carter's side become the last of the 92 clubs to concede a goal when Martin hits a second-half equaliser, after his first shot was saved by Connachan. The Boro goal stems from a Kaye cross, Harvey keeping out Horsfield's first effort, before being beaten by the follow-up.

No	Date		Att Pos	Pt	F-A	H-T	Scorers, Times, and Referees	1	2	3	4	5	6	7	8	9	10	11
4	5/9	A SOUTHAMPTON	13,989 17 15	L 3	0-2	0-2	Wimshurst 6, Sydenham 40 / Ref: R Aldous	Harvey	Foley	Everitt	Leck	Branston	Kiernan	Walden	Hunt	Livesey	Martin	Lines
								Hollowbread	*Williams*	*Hollywood*	*Wimshurst*	*Knapp*	*Huxford*	*Paine*	*McGuigan*	*Chivers*	*Burnside*	*Sydenham*

The temperature is in the 70s as the Cobblers trail early on – Wimshurst's shot going in off a post after he collected a return pass from Chivers. Sydenham rounds Foley before firing the second while Everitt's tough reputation is enhanced with a booking for a scything tackle on Paine.

No	Date		Att Pos	Pt	F-A	H-T	Scorers, Times, and Referees	1	2	3	4	5	6	7	8	9	10	11
5	8/9	H NEWCASTLE	15,977 12 7	W 5	1-0	0-0	Etheridge 82 / Ref: E Wells	Harvey	Foley	Everitt	Leck	Branston	Kiernan	Walden	Best	Livesey	Etheridge	Lines
								Marshall	*Craig*	*Clark*	*Anderson*	*McGrath*	*Moncur*	*Robson*	*Hilley*	*Thomas*	*McGarry*	*Hockey*

The season's first changes bring in Etheridge and Best for the injured Hunt and rested Martin. Lines has a goal disallowed for the second game running, but Etheridge inflicts the Magpies' first defeat with a close-range finish when Marshall can only block Livesey's shot on the turn.

No	Date		Att Pos	Pt	F-A	H-T	Scorers, Times, and Referees	1	2	3	4	5	6	7	8	9	10	11
6	11/9	H HUDDERSFIELD	12,984 10 19	W 7	3-2	2-1	Robson 15, 56, Livesey 40 / O'Grady 24, Massie 84 / Ref: V Batty	Harvey	Foley	Everitt	Leck	Branston	Kiernan	Walden	Best	Livesey	Etheridge	Robson
								Wood	*Parker*	*Meagan*	*Massie*	*Coddington*	*Dinsdale*	*Lewis*	*White*	*Gilliver*	*Balderstone*	*O'Grady*

Friday night avoids a clash with the following day's Town Show. Lines is missing with a thigh injury and his replacement Robson makes his presence felt with a header and a deft shot while Livesey's tremendous solo effort – capped by a 25-yard shot leaves the Terriers without a win.

No	Date		Att Pos	Pt	F-A	H-T	Scorers, Times, and Referees	1	2	3	4	5	6	7	8	9	10	11
7	15/9	A IPSWICH	13,520 11 22	D 8	0-0	0-0	Ref: N Burtenshaw	Harvey	Foley	Everitt	Leck	Branston	Kiernan	Walden	Best	Livesey	Etheridge	Robson
								Bailey	*Davin*	*Smith*	*Thrower*	*Bolton*	*Elsworthy*	*Stephenson*	*Hegan*	*Baker*	*Leadbetter*	*Brogan*

Ipswich are in turmoil after the resignation of Jackie Milburn, trainer Jimmy Forsyth in temporary charge. Harvey is the hero, saving a penalty after left-winger Brogan tumbles in the box in the 68th minute. Harvey blocks his shot and turns Leadbetter's follow-up effort around the post.

No	Date		Att Pos	Pt	F-A	H-T	Scorers, Times, and Referees	1	2	3	4	5	6	7	8	9	10	11
8	19/9	A COVENTRY	30,113 8 7	W 10	1-0	0-0	Robson 76 / Ref: G McCabe	Harvey	Foley	Everitt	Leck	Branston	Kiernan	Walden	Best	Livesey	Etheridge	Robson
								Wesson	*Sillett*	*Kearns*	*Bruck*	*Curtis*	*Farmer*	*Humphries*	*Hale*	*Kirby*	*Smith*	*Rees*

The Sky Blues' storming start is fast becoming a distant memory as this brings a fourth defeat on the trot after five wins. Jimmy Hill's 63-64 Division Three champions are turned over in a local derby which saw 17 coachloads and a special train of Cobblers fans make the short hop.

No	Date		Att Pos	Pt	F-A	H-T	Scorers, Times, and Referees	1	2	3	4	5	6	7	8	9	10	11
9	26/9	H CARDIFF	12,328 6 19	W 12	1-0	1-0	Everitt 25 / Ref: K Burns	Harvey	Foley	Everitt	Leck	Branston	Kiernan	Walden	Hunt	Livesey	Etheridge	Robson
								Wilson	*Rodrigues*	*Peck*	*Williams*	*Charles*	*Hole*	*King*	*Loyd*	*Tapscott*	*Allchurch*	*Lewis*

The terrace joke is that trainer Joe Payne is the only injury worry prior to this first Saturday home game. Everitt becomes the seventh Cobbler to score, when his 40-yard free kick deceived Wilson, leaving the Bluebirds without a win in 12 matches, despite six draws so far this season.

No	Date		Att Pos	Pt	F-A	H-T	Scorers, Times, and Referees	1	2	3	4	5	6	7	8	9	10	11
10	29/9	H IPSWICH	14,886 3 22	W 14	3-2	1-0	Hunt 37, 67, 72 / Colrain 69, Broadfoot 79 / Ref: W Gow	Harvey	Foley	Everitt	Leck	Branston	Kiernan	Walden	Hunt	Livesey	Etheridge	Robson
								Thorburn	*Carberry*	*McNeil*	*Blackwood*	*Bolton*	*Thrower*	*Broadfoot*	*Hegan*	*Colrain*	*Leadbetter*	*Brogan*

Almost at the top... Hunt's fine positional sense reaps hat-trick dividends. Livesey puts him through for his first and third goals, while headers by Livesey and Etheridge create his second – a header. Ipswich, 4-2 winners at Middlesbrough on the Saturday, return to the foot of the table.

11 A PRESTON 3/10

1	D	2-2	15,953	18	15

Walden 1, Robson 8
Dawson 5, Godfrey 30
Ref: P Baldwin

Harvey	Foley	Everitt	Leck	Branston	Kiernan	Walden	Hunt	Livesey	Etheridge	Robson
Kelly	*Ross*	*Smith*	*Lawton*	*Singleton*	*Kendall*	*Wilson*	*Godfrey*	*Dawson*	*Spavin*	*Holden*

Spavin passes a late fitness test to ensure Preston's line-up is the one beaten 2-3 by West Ham in the FA Cup final, with the exception of ex-Cobbler Alec Ashworth. After all the early drama, Hunt has an effort disallowed but in the second half the Cobblers' goal leads a charmed life.

---

12 A PORTSMOUTH 7/10

2	D	3-3	12,262	16	16

Robson 43, Livesey 49, Branston 88
Barton 15, 86, McCann 22
Ref: J Osborne

Harvey	Foley	Everitt	Leck	Branston	Kiernan	Walden	Hunt	Livesey	Etheridge	Robson
Milkins	*Cordjohn*	*Lumiss*	*Lewis*	*Dickinson*	*Harris*	*McClelland*	*Portwood*	*Tindall*	*McCann*	*Barton*

Pompey had won three home games without conceding a goal in the previous eighteen days and take a 2-0 lead in 22 minutes. Tony Barton, who manages the Cobblers years later, appears to have won it for George Smith's side but Branston pops up with a late headed point-saver.

---

13 H CHARLTON 10/10

1	W	1-0	13,552	3	18

Robson 55
Ref: P Hackney

Harvey	Foley	Cockcroft	Leck	Branston	Kiernan	Walden	Hunt	Livesey	Etheridge	Robson
Jones	*Hewie*	*Kinsey*	*Bailey*	*Tocknell*	*Edwards*	*Kenning*	*Durant*	*Matthews*	*Peacock*	*Glover*

The matchday programme congratulates boss Bowen on his recent appointment as Welsh team manager. Wales' 3-2 win over Scotland in Cardiff coincided with the draw at Preston. Cockcroft replaces the injured Everitt, whose run of 80 consecutive league games comes to an end.

---

14 A LEYTON ORIENT 17/10

1	D	2-2	8,390	13	19

Hall 10, Martin 74
Price 18, 48
Ref: P Rhodes

Harvey	Foley	Everitt	Leck	Branston	Kiernan	Walden	Martin	Livesey	Hall	Robson
Ramage	*Hollow*	*Webb*	*Ward*	*Nelson*	*Sorrell*	*Price*	*Phillips*	*Dunmore*	*Gregory*	*McDonald*

Harold Wilson has been returned to 10 Downing Street during a week the Russians blasted three cosmonauts into orbit. Then 19-year-old Jim Hall fires the Cobblers' meteoric rise, scoring from 20 yards. The O's, crushed 5-0 at Newcastle the previous Saturday, prove tougher at home.

---

15 H BURY 24/10

1	W	2-0	11,324	15	21

Foley 55p, Martin 59
Ref: G Martin

Harvey	Foley	Everitt	Leck	Branston	Kiernan	Walden	Martin	Livesey	Hall	Robson
Harker	*Gallagher*	*Eastham*	*Turner*	*Bunner*	*Atherton*	*Leech*	*Griffin*	*Alston*	*Bell*	*Parry*

The sides met for the first time in 1963-64, but this brings an inaugural win over The Shakers, managed by Bob Stokoe. In the Bury line-up is Colin Bell, later to become an unsuccessful transfer target for Bowen. Kurila turns down the chance to move to Walsall after a fee is agreed.

---

16 A CRYSTAL PALACE 31/10

1	W	2-1	21,331	9	23

Robson 60, Livesey 85
Holton 84
Ref: R Aldous

Harvey	Foley	Everitt	Leck	Branston	Kiernan	Walden	Martin	Livesey	Hunt	Robson
Millington	*Sewell*	*Townsend*	*Whitehouse*	*Stephenson*	*Howe*	*Werge*	*Burridge*	*Holton*	*Kellard*	*Dowsett*

Palace have booked a fourth round League Cup trip to eventual runners-up Leicester (beaten 2-3 by Chelsea). Ex-Cobbler Cliff Holton treats his old teammates to one of his specials, a long-range rocket which briefly threatens to rock the boat before Livesey heads the late winner.

---

17 H NORWICH 7/11

1	D	0-0	16,774	3	24

Ref: J Cooke

Harvey	Foley	Everitt	Leck	Branston	Kiernan	Walden	Martin	Livesey	Hunt	Robson
Keelan	*Kelly*	*Mullett*	*Lucas*	*Sharpe*	*Hill*	*Shaw*	*Bolland*	*Davies*	*Bryceland*	*Punton*

The Cobblers are eyeing a fifth round League Cup-tie at Plymouth or Division One side Stoke, last season's beaten finalists, after the sides drew 1-1. This is Hunt's last match for over four months as he succumbs to cartilage trouble. A fast-reviving Ipswich thrash Portsmouth 7-0.

---

18 A ROTHERHAM 14/11

1	D	1-1	11,273	10	25

Leck 17
Butler 67
Ref: W Crossley

Harvey	Foley	Everitt	Leck	Branston	Kiernan	Best	Martin	Livesey	Lines	Robson
Ironside	*Carver*	*Clish*	*Lambert*	*Madden*	*Jackson*	*Lyons*	*Casper*	*Tiler*	*Houghton*	*Butler*

An experiment sees Lines play at inside-left but it is an over-worked defence who earn their corn, with Branston outstanding, as The Millers miss lots of chances. Leck collects a Robson pass to score from outside the box but Butler breaks the offside trap to score a deserved equaliser.

---

19 H SWANSEA 21/11

1	W	2-1	13,427	20	27

Robson 11, Martin 65
Kirby 22
Ref: R Harper

Harvey	Foley	Everitt	Leck	Branston	Kiernan	Walden	Martin	Livesey	Lines	Robson
Dwyer	*Hughes*	*Ward*	*Hayes*	*Johnson*	*Williams*	*Evans*	*Thomas*	*Kirby*	*Todd*	*McLaughlin*

Swansea had won their previous four games at the County Ground and this is a first win over the Welshmen for 41 years. Walden, back for Best, beats two men and when his shot is saved by Dwyer, Robson fires in the loose ball. Everitt's late goal-line clearance ensures the bonus.

---

20 A DERBY 28/11

1	D	2-2	17,367	8	28

Martin 33, Brown 85
Durban 11, Buxton 51
Ref: F Cowan

Harvey	Foley	Cockcroft	Leck	Branston	Kiernan	Walden	Martin	Livesey	Brown	Robson
Matthews	*Barrowcliffe*	*Ferguson*	*Webster*	*Young*	*Parry*	*Hughes*	*Boners*	*Buxton*	*Durban*	*Curry*

Alan Durban is to become a frequent thorn to Cobblers' sides. Here, he is in only his second season at the Baseball Ground, before playing more than 300 games in nine years. County's other goal comes from sporting all-rounder Ian Buxton, who turned out at cricket for Derbyshire.

---

21 H SWINDON 5/12

1	W	2-1	9,586	21	30

Robson 72, Brown 75
Brown 62
Ref: E Crawford

Harvey	Foley	Cockcroft	Leck	Branston	Kiernan	Walden	Brown	Livesey	Martin	Robson
Hicks	*Dawson*	*Trollope*	*Morgan*	*Hallett*	*Sproates*	*Summerbee*	*Shergold*	*East*	*Brown*	*Rogers*

Swindon had come up with the Cobblers in 1962-63 and include names etched in folklore, such as Summerbee, Rogers and Trollope, the latter playing 767 times for the club, and whose son turned out in a claret shirt years later. Brown's winner is a terrific left-foot drive from 30 yards.

LEAGUE DIVISION 2 — Manager: Dave Bowen — SEASON 1964-65

No	Date			Att	Pos	Pt	F-A	H-T	Scorers, Times, and Referees
22	12/12	A	NEWCASTLE	40,376	1	30	0-5 L	0-4	[Everitt 45 (og)] / Hockey 7, McGarry 43, 44, 89; Ref: C Cooke

Pos	1	2	3	4	5	6	7	8	9	10	11
Northampton	Harvey	Foley	Everitt	Leek	Branston	Kiernan	Walden	Brown	Livesey	Martin	Robson
Newcastle	Marshall	Craig	Clark	Anderson	McGrath	Iley	Hockey	Hilley	McGarry	Penman	Suddick

Morpeth-born Robson has an unhappy homecoming, stretchered off after 15 minutes with a head injury, an incident which acts as a catalyst to the end of the 'run' with a calamitous three-minute spell before half-time erasing the memory of a 3-2 victory here during the previous season.

No	Date			Att	Pos	Pt	F-A	H-T	Scorers, Times, and Referees
23	19/12	H	MANCHESTER C	12,665	12	32	2-0 W	0-0	Leek 79, Everitt 83; Ref: A Fussey

Pos	1	2	3	4	5	6	7	8	9	10	11
Northampton	Harvey	Foley	Cockcroft	Leek	Branston	Kiernan	Walden	Everitt	Livesey	Leek	Lines
Manchester C	Dowd	Bacuzzi	Sear	Kennedy	Batty	Oakes	Wagstaffe	Gray	Murray	Kevan	Young

Robson has suffered concussion, a broken jaw and lost three teeth at Newcastle, so Lines returns, while Everitt and Leek, signed for £10,000 from Birmingham the previous week, are the new inside-forwards. A first double of the season, and a repeat scoreline of that at Maine Road.

No	Date			Att	Pos	Pt	F-A	H-T	Scorers, Times, and Referees
24	26/12	A	BOLTON	24,487	4	33	0-0 D	0-0	Ref: D Payne

Pos	1	2	3	4	5	6	7	8	9	10	11
Northampton	Harvey	Foley	Cockcroft	Leek	Branston	Kiernan	Walden	Everitt	Livesey	Leek	Robson
Bolton	Hopkinson	Cooper	Farrimond	Rimmer	Edwards	Hatton	Lee	Hill	Davies	Bromley	Taylor

Bolton have not lost in the league since October and they are managed by ex-Cobbler Bill Ridding but this is an ill-tempered affair which sees Syd Farrimond booked for kicking the ball away, while at the end of the contest two youths run onto the pitch and try to attack the referee.

No	Date			Att	Pos	Pt	F-A	H-T	Scorers, Times, and Referees
25	2/1	H	SOUTHAMPTON	15,245	6	34	2-2 D	1-1	Leek 4, Branston 74 / Chivers 28, Foley 72 (og); Ref: W Clements

Pos	1	2	3	4	5	6	7	8	9	10	11
Northampton	Harvey	Foley	Cockcroft	Leek	Branston	Kiernan	Walden	Everitt	Livesey	Leek	Robson
Southampton	Hollowbread	Williams	Hollywood	Wimeshurst	Knapp	Hurford	Paine	O'Brien	Chivers	Melia	Chadwick

The Bolton return is postponed but the pitch recovers for Harvey to save two penalties from Paine. The joy of the second is brief, as Foley heads the resultant corner into his own net. Branston, whose goals have a habit of being equalisers against south-coast clubs, comes up trumps.

No	Date			Att	Pos	Pt	F-A	H-T	Scorers, Times, and Referees
26	16/1	A	HUDDERSFIELD	7,359	21	34	0-2 L	0-2	Balderstone 20, Massie 39; Ref: C Duxbury

Pos	1	2	3	4	5	6	7	8	9	10	11
Northampton	Harvey	Foley	Everitt	Leek	Branston	Kiernan	Walton	Martin	Brown	Leek	Robson
Huddersfield	Wood	Atkins	Meagan	Nicholson	Coddington	Dinsdale	McHale	Massie	Leighton	Balderstone	O'Grady

England international Ray Wood denies Brown with three great saves as winger Kevin McHale wallows like a hippo, revelling in the churned up mud. At least the Cobblers don't lose ground at the top, as Newcastle lose 4-5 at Coventry while Norwich go down 0-2 at Crystal Palace.

No	Date			Att	Pos	Pt	F-A	H-T	Scorers, Times, and Referees
27	23/1	H	COVENTRY	18,741	8	35	1-1 D	1-0	Leek 31 / Clements 73; Ref: R Egan

Pos	1	2	3	4	5	6	7	8	9	10	11
Northampton	Harvey	Foley	Everitt	Leek	Branston	Kiernan	Lines	Martin	Brown	Leek	Robson
Coventry	Wesson	Hill	Harris	Bruck	Curtis	Kearns	Humphries	Hale	Hudson	Clements	Rees

Pop band The King Bees entertain the crowd pitch-side for an hour before kick-off. Both goals are scored by players who had asked to be dropped, with Leek opening things up after Brown's effort is saved by Wesson while there is a suspicion of offside about the Clements' strike.

No	Date			Att	Pos	Pt	F-A	H-T	Scorers, Times, and Referees
28	6/2	A	CARDIFF	7,427	18	37	2-0 W	0-0	Brown 48, 65; Ref: A Edge

Pos	1	2	3	4	5	6	7	8	9	10	11
Northampton	Harvey	Wilson	Everitt	Leek	Branston	Kiernan	Walden	Martin	Brown	Leek	Robson
Cardiff		Harrington	Rodrigues	Williams	Murray	Hole	Farrell	King	Charles	Tapscott	Lewis

City suffer a European Cup-Winners' Cup quarter-final hangover. They had lost 0-1 to Real Zaragoza a few days earlier, after drawing 2-2 in Spain in the first leg. Here, they are undone by a player who would later join them, Brown converting incisive passes by Robson and Leek.

No	Date			Att	Pos	Pt	F-A	H-T	Scorers, Times, and Referees
29	13/2	H	PRESTON	14,010	8	39	2-1 W	1-1	Brown 2, Robson 66 / Godfrey 11; Ref: G Powell

Pos	1	2	3	4	5	6	7	8	9	10	11
Northampton	Harvey	Kelly	Everitt	Leek	Branston	Kurila	Walden	Martin	Brown	Leek	Robson
Preston	Ross	Smith	Lawton	Singleton	Cranston	Wilson	Godfrey	Dawson	Spavin	Holden	

This is the only league match Kiernan misses for two seasons, with Kurila taking his place in a line-up which buries a bogey, as Preston had twice knocked the Cobblers out of cup-ties in the post-war era, while also completing a league double over Bowen's men the previous season.

No	Date			Att	Pos	Pt	F-A	H-T	Scorers, Times, and Referees
30	20/2	A	CHARLTON	8,956	15	40	1-1 D	0-1	Robson 47 / Kennedy 41; Ref: G Roper

Pos	1	2	3	4	5	6	7	8	9	10	11
Northampton	Harvey	Rose	Everitt	Leek	Branston	Kiernan	Walden	Martin	Brown	Leek	Robson
Charlton	Bonds	Kinsey	Hewie	Haydock	Tocknall	Kenning	Kennedy	Matthews	Firman	Peacock	

The Cobblers trail to a deflected shot while Brown's header is superbly saved by Rose. But they almost snatch a win as Walden's effort lobs onto the bar two minutes from time. Promotion rivals Bolton are beaten 0-1 at Bolton, while eventual winners Liverpool in the 5th round of the FA Cup.

No	Date			Att	Pos	Pt	F-A	H-T	Scorers, Times, and Referees
31	27/2	H	LEYTON ORIENT	13,517	1	42	2-0 W	1-0	Leek 3, Robson 50; Ref: R Starling

Pos	1	2	3	4	5	6	7	8	9	10	11
Northampton	Harvey	Rammage	Everitt	Leek	Branston	Kiernan	Walden	Martin	Brown	Leek	Robson
Leyton Orient	Charlton	Worrell	Farrell	Nelson	Harris	Elwood	Gregory	Dunmore	Metchick	Musgrove	

Orient did the Cobblers a huge favour a week earlier, beating Newcastle 2-1 at Brisbane Road, and this win, combined with another Magpies loss (2-3 at home to Bury) and a 2-5 drubbing for Norwich at Bolton, sees Bowen's men return to the top for the first time since 12 December.

No		Opponent	Date	Pos	Res		Pts	Att	Score	Scorers	Ref
32	H	BOLTON	2/3	1	W	5	44	15,515	2-0	Martin 4, 85 Foley 12, Leck 49	Ref: P Brandwood
33	H	CRYSTAL PALACE	13/3	2	D	6	45	17,350	1-1	Brown 17 / Cutler 2	Ref: J Taylor
34	A	NORWICH	20/3	2	D	3	46	25,199	1-1	Robson 25 / Alcock 30	Ref: K Stokes
35	A	SWINDON	23/3	2	L	18	46	17,886	2-4	Brown 6, 40 [Rogers 86] / Hunt 48, 60 Summerbee 50	Ref: G Martin
36	H	ROTHERHAM	27/3	2	W	13	48	19,488	1-0	Brown 35	Ref: R Spittles
37	A	SWANSEA	3/4	2	W	22	50	10,516	2-1	Martin 5, Brown 53 / Todd 28	Ref: J Finney
38	H	DERBY	10/4	2	D	5	51	17,917	2-2	Martin 58, Brown 76 / Durban 75, 80	Ref: E Crawford
39	A	BURY	17/4	2	W	16	53	6,800	4-1	Kiernan 5, Brown 14, Martin 39, 58 / Durrant 21	Ref: P Baldwin
40	A	PLYMOUTH	19/4	2	L	11	53	10,547	2-5	Kiernan 22, Martin 78 [Newm'n 67] / Reyn'ds 9, J'kson 32, 56, Will'ms 41p	Ref: H New
41	H	PLYMOUTH	20/4	2	W	12	55	19,718	3-1	Newman 40 (og), Martin 58 / Reynolds 88 [Brown 70]	Ref: W Handley
42	H	PORTSMOUTH	24/4	2	D	20	56	20,660	0-0	Gordon 77 (og) / Wilson 84	Ref: R Boyles

Home Average 15,366 Away 16,753

Line-ups (Cobblers / opponents) and match reports

32 — Bolton 2-0: Harvey/Hopkinson, Foley/Hartle, Everitt/Farrimond, Leck/Rimmer, Branston/Edwards, Kiernan/Hatton, Walden/Lee, Martin/Hill, Brown/Davies, Leek/Bromley, Robson/Taylor
It is another four years before the Cobblers win a league match by four clear goals, and this becomes an occasion to savour. It includes a swirling 40-yard free-kick by Foley which deceives Hopkinson, a 25-yard special by Leck, and another Harvey penalty save, from Lee's kick.

33 — Crystal Palace 1-1: Harvey/Jackson, Foley/Long, Everitt/Wood, Leck/Holesgrove, Branston/Stephenson, Kiernan/Burnside, Walden/Whitehouse, Martin/Burridge, Brown/Cutler, Leek/Smith, Robson/Kellard
Kiernan's early headed back-pass is intercepted by Cutler who runs on to fire Palace ahead, but when Brown converts a Martin cross, another home win looks likely. Palace cling on for a point though, and Newcastle return to the top after registering a 2-0 home victory over Norwich.

34 — Norwich 1-1: Harvey/Keelan!, Foley/Kelly, Everitt/Mullett, Leck/Lucas, Branston/Butler, Kiernan/Sutton, Walden/Heath, Martin/Bryceland, Brown/Alcock, Leek/Davies, Robson/Punton
How many teeth does Robson have left? Two more are knocked out as Keelan's right hook reduces the Canaries to ten men in a bad-tempered affair, with Leck and Branston booked, and the latter carried off with a knee injury which ends his season. Harvey saves Mullett's penalty kick.

35 — Swindon 2-4: Harvey/Oakley, Foley/Dawson, Everitt/Trollope, Leck/Smart, Carr/McPherson, Kiernan/Atherton, Walden/Summerbee, Martin/Hunt, Brown/Hunt, Hall/Atkins, Robson/Rogers
Carr replaces Branston, and Hall comes in for the injured Leck but, although Hall has a goal ruled out by a linesman's flag, the Cobblers can have no complaints as the loss of their linchpin centre-half is instantly apparent, with the early second-half turnaround by Bert Head's side.

36 — Rotherham 1-0: Harvey/Morritt, Foley/Carver, Everitt/Clish, Leck/Lambert, Carr/Madden, Kiernan/Hardy, Walden/Lyons, Martin/Bennett, Brown/Galley, Hall/Tiler, Robson/Casper
A Saturday evening kick-off allows Cobblers fans to enjoy Jay Trump's afternoon Grand National victory at Aintree. Supporters pay tribute to chairman Fred York who had died three days earlier. Leck makes his 250th league appearance while the attendance is the largest in four years.

37 — Swansea 2-1: Harvey/Briggs, Foley/Evans, Everitt/Hughes, Leck/Harley, Carr/Johnson, Kiernan/Davies, Walden/Humphries, Martin/Todd, Brown/Kirby, Hall/McGugan, Robson/McLaughlin
Promotion is looking increasingly likely after this first ever Cobblers win at the Vetch Field. Nine previous visits stretching back to 1919 had brought four draws and five defeats. Rivals Bolton and Norwich are beaten, 0-3 at Portsmouth and 0-2 at home to Huddersfield respectively.

38 — Derby 2-2: Harvey/Boulton, Foley/Barrowcliffe, Everitt/Ferguson, Leck/Webster, Carr/Young, Kiernan/Parry, Walden/Hughes, Martin/Thomas, Brown/Buxton, Hall/Durban, Robson/Bowers
That man Durban again proves a fly in the ointment. His side had won by the only goal at the County Ground in 1963-64 and despite Martin's header and another Brown goal against The Rams, kept the momentum going. This was to be Derby's last point earned until 4 September.

39 — Bury 4-1: Harvey/Harker, Foley/Gallagher, Everitt/Eastham, Leck/Leech, Carr/Bunner, Kiernan/Lindsay, Walden/Griffin, Martin/Yard, Brown/Alston, Hunt/Bell, Robson/Durrant
Cobblers first goal of the season set the ball rolling and the excellent Martin took his tally to four in three games. A champagne moment.

40 — Plymouth 2-5: Harvey/Leiper, Foley/Baird, Everitt/Piper, Leck!/Williams, Carr/Newman, Kiernan/Sanderson, Walden/Jones, Martin/Jackson, Brown/Lord, Hunt/Reynolds, Robson/Jennings
Kiernan's first goal of the season was the proud headline to scream from the front page of the Saturday night Green 'Un after this stylish success. For the first time in the club's history the Cobblers fly to an English game, but the Easter experience is not a happy one. Leck is sent off in the 24th-minute after an incident involving Argyle's 16-year-old inside-forward Richard Reynolds, while Walden and Foley concede penalties.

41 — Plymouth 3-1: Harvey/Dwyer, Foley/Baird, Everitt/Hore, Leck/Neal, Carr/Newman, Kiernan/Williams, Walden/Jones, Martin/Lord, Brown/Reynolds, Hunt/Sanderson, Robson/Jennings
It becomes a race back to Northampton for the second meeting in just over 24 hours, this being an Easter Tuesday evening celebration of promotion to Division One. Hunt has a goal disallowed as the Cobblers keep alive their chance of pipping Newcastle to the Division Two title.

42 — Portsmouth 0-0: Harvey/Armstrong, Foley/Wilson, Everitt/Tindall, Leck/Gordon, Carr/Dickinson, Kiernan/Harris, Walden/McClelland, Martin/McCann, Brown/Edwards, Hunt/Portwood, Robson/Barton
Swindon's afternoon defeat at Southampton leaves Portsmouth needing a point to stay in Division Two on the day football legend Jimmy Dickinson retires on his 40th birthday. The Cobblers preserve their unbeaten home record despite Wilson's goal, which dribbles over the line.

LEAGUE DIVISION 2 (CUP-TIES) Manager: Dave Bowen SEASON 1964-65

League Cup

Match	F-A	H-T	Scorers, Times, and Referees	1	2	3	4	5	6	7	8	9	10	11
2 A BOURNEMOUTH 8 W 23/9 8,807 3:16	2-0	1-0	Walden 34, Hunt 87 Ref: A Weller	Harvey *Best*	Foley *Farmer*	Everitt *Compton*	Leck *Groves*	Branston *Nelson*	Kiernan *Bolton !*	Walden *Bomstead*	Hunt *Woods*	Livesey *Reeves*	Etheridge *Archer*	Robson *Coxan*
3 H PORTSMOUTH 1 W 20/10 7,380 2:19	2-1	2-0	Livesey 6, Martin 44 *Barton 61* Ref: W Handrey	Harvey *Milkins*	Foley *Cordjohn*	Everitt *Lunniss*	Leck *Lewis*	Branston *Dickinson*	Kiernan *Harris*	Walden *McClelland*	Martin *Portwood*	Livesey *Tindall*	Hall *McCann*	Robson *Barton*
4 H CHESTERFIELD 1 W 4/11 6,695 4:13	4-1	2-0	Martin 35, 85, Hunt 25, Foley 90p *Clarke 52p* Ref: P Brandwood	Powell *Holmes*	Foley *Sears*	Everitt ! *Clarke*	Leck *Phelan*	Branston *Beresford*	Kiernan *Duncan*	Walden *Stringfellow*	Hunt *Commons*	Livesey *Hughes*	Martin *McCann*	Robson
QF A PLYMOUTH 1 L 25/11 21,698 2:3	0-1	0-1	*Newman 8* Ref: J Finney	Harvey *Maclaren*	Foley *Book*	Cockcroft *Reeves*	Kurila *Newman*	Branston *Neale*	Kiernan *Jackson*	Walden *Jones*	Brown *Trebilcock*	Walden *Lord*	Hall *Sanderson*	Lines *Jennings*

Referee Weller needs a police escort after booking, and then sending off the Cherries' left-half Bolton, while he also books Branston for a foul on Reeves. Bournemouth had beaten Luton 4-0 in Division Three on the Saturday but Walden's six-yard shot and Hunt's neat header seal it.

The County Ground faithful give their heroes a standing ovation at half-time but shuffle from the terraces on 90 minutes puzzled by what then follows, as the Cobblers survive an examination, and are lucky to reach the fourth round of the League Cup for the first time in their history.

Everitt's sending-off five minutes before the break for a retaliatory kick at right-winger Duncan makes life tough, especially when Leck fouls skipper Commons, allowing Clarke to make it 2-1 from the penalty spot. The Cobblers' penalty arrives after Holmes fouls Walden in the box.

The offside trap proves a dismal failure as Neale breaks through early on, his pass allowing Newman to round Harvey before slotting into the unguarded net. Plymouth stretch their unbeaten home run to 20 games, while this was the Cobblers' first league or cup slip up in 19 matches.

FA Cup

Match	F-A	H-T	Scorers, Times, and Referees	1	2	3	4	5	6	7	8	9	10	11
3 A CHELSEA 2 L 9/1 44,335 1:2	1-4	0-1	*[Foley 59, og]* Foley 70p *Tambling 44, Bridges 57, 77,* Ref: T Dawes	Harvey *Bonetti*	Foley *Hinton*	Cockcroft *Harris*	Leck *Hollins*	Branston *Mortimore*	Kiernan *Upton*	Walden *Murray*	Everitt *Graham*	Livesey *Bridges*	Leek *Venables*	Robson *Tambling*

Chelsea had already hit five at home to Blackburn and Everton this season and had scored four at home to Leicester the previous week, so this was no disgrace. Robson tested Bonetti early on and played a blinder, a fact which stuck in Tommy Docherty's mind until he later signed him.

League Table

Team	P	Home					Away					Pts
		W	D	L	F	A	W	D	L	F	A	
1 Newcastle	42	16	4	1	50	16	8	5	8	31	29	57
2 NORTHTON	42	14	7	0	37	16	6	9	6	29	34	56
3 Bolton	42	13	6	2	46	17	7	4	10	34	41	50
4 Southampton	42	12	6	3	49	25	5	8	8	34	38	48
5 Ipswich	42	11	7	3	48	30	4	10	7	26	37	47
6 Norwich	42	15	4	2	47	21	3	3	13	14	36	47
7 Crystal Pal	42	11	6	4	37	24	5	7	9	18	27	45
8 Huddersfield	42	12	4	5	28	15	6	6	10	25	36	44
9 Derby	42	11	5	5	48	35	6	6	10	36	44	43
10 Coventry	42	10	5	6	41	29	4	6	11	31	41	43
11 Manchester C	42	12	3	6	40	24	4	4	13	23	38	41
12 Preston	42	11	8	2	46	29	3	5	13	30	52	41
13 Cardiff	42	10	7	4	43	25	3	7	11	21	32	40
14 Rotherham	42	10	7	4	39	25	4	5	12	31	44	40
15 Plymouth	42	10	7	4	36	28	1	6	14	27	51	40
16 Bury	42	9	4	8	36	30	5	6	10	24	36	38
17 Middlesbro	42	8	5	8	40	31	4	4	12	30	45	35
18 Charlton	42	8	5	8	35	34	5	4	12	29	41	35
19 Leyton Orient	42	10	4	7	36	34	2	7	12	14	38	35
20 Portsmouth	42	11	4	6	36	22	1	6	14	20	55	34
21 Swindon	42	12	3	6	43	30	2	3	17	20	51	33
22 Swansea	42	9	7	5	40	29	2	3	16	22	55	32
	924	245	118	99	901	569	99	118	245	569	901	924

Odds & ends

Double wins: (4) Manchester City, Cardiff, Bury, Swansea.
Double losses: (0).

Won from behind: (1) Swindon (h)
Lost from in front: (1) Swindon (a).

High spots: A 17-match unbeaten league run between 8 September and 12 December, beginning and ending against Newcastle United.
The club reaches the quarter-finals of the League Cup for the first time.
Equalling the feat of 1932-33, remaining unbeaten at home all season.
Goalkeeper Bryan Harvey saves six penalties.

Low spots: Failing by two points (Newcastle had a better goal-average) to win the title, despite losing three fewer games than the Magpies.
Crashing spectacularly in that league match at St James' Park.
Losing a 0-2 half-time lead at Swindon.
Attendances at home are criticised for failing to match the fine results.

Ever-presents: (3) Harvey, Foley, Leck
Hat-tricks: (1) Hunt.
Leading scorer: Martin (16).

Appearances and Goals

	Appearances			Goals			
	Lge	LC	FAC	Lge	LC	FAC	Tot
Best, Billy	4						
Branston, Terry	34	4	1	2			2
Brown, Bobby	20	1		13			13
Carr, Graham	8						
Cockroft, Vic	6	1	1				
Etheridge, Brian	9			1			1
Everitt, Mike	39	3	1	2			2
Foley, Theo	42	4	1	3	1	1	5
Hall, Jim	6	2		1			1
Harvey, Bryan	42	4	1				
Hunt, Bobby	16	2		4	2		6
Kiernan, Joe	41	4	1	2			2
Kurila, John	1	1					
Leck, Derek	42	3	1	3			3
Leek, Ken	12			3			3
Lines, Barry	9	1					
Livesey, Charlie	25	4	1	3	2		5
Martin, Don	30	2	1	13	3		16
Robson, Tommy	36	3	1	13			13
Walden, Harry	39	4	1	1			1
Walton, Ronnie	1						
(own-goals)				2			2
21 players used	462	44	11	66	8	1	75

LEAGUE DIVISION 1 — Manager: Dave Bowen — SEASON 1965-66

No		Date	Att	Pos		Pt	F-A	H-T	Scorers, Times, and Referees
1	A EVERTON	21/8	48,489	21 *2*	L	0	2-5	1-1	Brown 24, Hunt 80 [Temple 72, 88] Young 20, Pickering 69, 82, Ref: J Carr
2	H ARSENAL	25/8	17,352	17 *7*	D	1	1-1	0-1	Brown 57 / Baldwin 18, Ref: K Howley
3	H MANCHESTER U	28/8	21,245	20 *12*	D	2	1-1	0-1	Hunt 83 / Connelly 10, Ref: D Brady
4	A NEWCASTLE	4/9	28,051	21 *10*	L	2	0-2	0-0	Suddick 47, Cummings 62, Ref: A Sparling
5	A BURNLEY	7/9	14,792	22 *3*	L	2	1-4	0-1	Livesey 63 / Foley 18 (og), Irvine 55, 81, 89, Ref: E Crawford
6	H WEST BROM	10/9	18,528	22 *1*	L	2	3-4	2-2	Lines 12, Robson 16, 82 / Hope 5, Astle 11, 55, 66, Ref: J Bullough
7	H BURNLEY	15/9	19,336	22 *1*	L	2	1-2	0-0	Robson 52 / Irvine 53, Elder 86, Ref: W Holian
8	A NOTT'M FOREST	18/9	19,669	21 *15*	D	3	1-1	1-0	Cockcroft 26 / Kear 89, Ref: H Richards
9	H SHEFFIELD WED	25/9	16,299	21 *16*	D	4	0-0	0-0	Ref: G Roper
10	A ARSENAL	28/9	33,240	21 *9*	D	5	1-1	0-0	Hall 63 / Radford 60, Ref: N Burtenshaw

Line-ups (opponents in *italics*)

Match	1	2	3	4	5	6	7	8	9	10	11	12 sub used
1 EVERTON	Harvey	Foley	Everitt	Kurila	Branston	Kiernan	Walden	Hunt	Brown	Lines	Robson	
Everton	*West*	*Wright*	*Wilson*	*Gabriel*	*Labone*	*Harris*	*Scott*	*Harvey*	*Pickering*	*Young*	*Temple*	
2 ARSENAL	Harvey	Foley	Everitt*	Leck	Carr	Kiernan	Walden	Hunt	Brown	Lines	Robson	Cockcroft
Arsenal	*Wilson*	*Howe*	*McCullough*	*Neill*	*Ure*	*McLintock*	*Baldwin*	*Eastham*	*Baker*	*Court*	*Armstrong*	
3 MANCHESTER U	Harvey	Foley	Cockcroft	Leck	Carr	Kiernan	Walden	Hunt	Brown	Lines	Robson	
Manchester U	*Gaskell*	*Dunne*	*Cantwell*	*Crerand*	*Foulkes*	*Stiles*	*Connelly*	*Charlton*	*Herd*	*Law*	*Best*	
4 NEWCASTLE	Harvey	Foley	Cockcroft	Leck	Carr	Kiernan	Walden	Hunt	Brown	Lines	Robson	
Newcastle	*Marshall*	*Craig*	*Clark*	*Anderson*	*McGrath*	*Iley*	*Hockey**	*McGarry*	*Cummings*	*Hilley*	*Suddick*	*Burton*
5 BURNLEY	Harvey	Thomson	Cockcroft	Leck	Carr	Kiernan*	Walden	Hunt	Brown	Livesey	Lines	Everitt
Burnley	*Thomson*	*Angus*	*Elder*	*O'Neil*	*Talbut*	*Miller*	*Morgan*	*Lochhead*	*Irvine*	*Bellamy*	*Harris*	
6 WEST BROM	Harvey	Foley	Everitt	Leck	Branston	Kiernan	Best	Livesey	Brown	Lines	Robson	
West Brom	*Potter*	*Cram*	*Williams*	*Howshall*	*Jones*	*Fraser*	*Foggo**	*Astle*	*Kaye*	*Hope*	*Brown*	*Lovett*
7 BURNLEY	Harvey	Thomson	Everitt	Leck	Carr	Kiernan	Best	Livesey	Brown	Lines	Robson	
Burnley	*Thomson*	*Angus*	*Elder*	*O'Neil*	*Talbut*	*Miller*	*Morgan*	*Lochhead*	*Irvine*	*Harris*	*Bellamy*	
8 NOTT'M FOREST	Harvey	Foley	Cockcroft	Kurila	Carr	Kiernan	Everitt	Hall	Brown	Lines	Robson	
Nott'm Forest	*Grummitt*	*Hindley**	*Machan*	*Newton*	*McKinlay*	*Whitefoot*	*Kear*	*Addison*	*Wignall*	*Barnwell*	*Hinton*	*Winfield*
9 SHEFFIELD WED	Harvey	Foley	Cockcroft	Kurila	Carr	Kiernan	Everitt	Martin	Brown	Lines	Robson	
Sheffield Wed	*Springett*	*Smith*	*Megson*	*Eustace*	*Mobley*	*Young*	*Usher*	*Quinn*	*Hickton*	*Fantham*	*Dobson*	
10 ARSENAL	Harvey	Foley	Everitt	Kurila	Carr	Kiernan	Walden	Martin	Hall	Lines	Robson	
Arsenal	*Furnell*	*Howe*	*McCullough*	*McLintock*	*Neill*	*Court*	*Armstrong*	*Radford*	*Baker*	*Sammels**	*Eastham*	*Skirton*

Match reports

1 — Everton (A). Everton possess eight full or Under-23 internationals in their side – a measure of what is to come, in front of the biggest crowd to see the Cobblers in Division One. Branston passes a fitness test on a bruised ankle but when this recurs, Bowen's men are exposed defensively late on.

2 — Arsenal (H). Brown and Bob Wilson are old buddies from their days together as amateur internationals and Wilson comes in for the injured Jim Furnell, his first outing at senior level for almost three years. Brown heads past him after a cross from Cockcroft, the Cobblers' first ever substitute used.

3 — Manchester U (H). The mighty Red Devils are not impressed at being asked to parade their wealth of skills in such an unlikely arena: 'how can you possibly play football in a place like this?' Denis Law is reputed to have asked. Connelly's goal has an offside look to it, as he latched onto Charlton's pass.

4 — Newcastle (A). Harvey admits to 'the biggest mistake of my life' for Suddick's opener, after efforts by Hunt and Brown beat Marshall, but are scooped off the line. McGrath saves an own-goal when Craig's back-pass beats his goalkeeper. Hilley's cross hits Carr and falls to Cummings for the second.

5 — Burnley (A). Foley's early own-goal comes against his old club after Hunt misses a golden chance, saved by Harry Thomson. After Kiernan limps off in the 50th minute, Willie Morgan rips the Cobblers apart and Willie Irvine collects three of his 29 season haul which sees him top the scoring charts.

6 — West Brom (H). Statistics abound… Astle's hat-trick gives him seven goals inside a week in this first ever meeting between these clubs, while Lines becomes the first man to score in all four divisions for the same club. A first home loss since the 1-2 defeat by Grimsby at the end of the 1963-4 season.

7 — Burnley (H). Thirty seconds of joy as the Cobblers lead for the first time this season. Burnley though, are made of serious stuff, having gone top with a 3-0 win over Manchester Utd at Turf Moor on the Saturday. The Clarets also strike the woodwork twice but Best is denied by Thomson's late save.

8 — Nott'm Forest (A). The Cobblers are now adopting a steely 4-3-3 formation and it comes within 90 seconds of producing a win dividend. Does Kear's equaliser from a corner go in with a hand? Forest forwards confess as much, as Cockcroft's only ever Cobblers goal, a 20-yard volley, is cancelled out.

9 — Sheffield Wed (H). Martin, injured in pre-season, replaces Hall to make his Division One debut in the heavy rain. Star of the show is Ron Springett who celebrates his England recall by playing a blinder, making two great saves from Lines. Liverpool race to a 5-0 win over Everton in the Merseyside derby.

10 — Arsenal (A). Arsenal had beaten Manchester Utd 4-2 on the Saturday but this could have been better for the Cobblers if Hall had not seen a 'winner' ruled out by Norman Burtenshaw, while another Hall effort flashes just wide in the dying minutes. The goal is a classic header from a Kiernan cross.

Match 11 — A LEICESTER, 2/10 — 21 D 1:1 (0-1) — 27,484 — 14 6
- Foley 47p / Goodfellow 28
- Ref: K Dagnall
- Northampton: Harvey, Foley, Everitt, Kurila*, Carr, Kiernan, Walden, Martin, Hall, Lines, Robson, Branston
- Leicester: Banks, Sjoberg, Norman, Roberts, King, Appleton, Sinclair, McDermott, Goodfellow, Gibson, Robson, Stringfellow

Manager Bowen watches the Cobblers rather than his Welsh side draw 0-0 with England and, in both cases, the goalkeeping heroics of Springett and Banks deny him. 'We won't meet Banks every week.' Walden is tripped for the penalty to revive the local derby travellers.

Match 12 — H SHEFFIELD UTD, 9/10 — 22 L 0-1 (0-1) — 17,300 — 1 6
- Mallender 10
- Ref: J Burns
- Northampton: Harvey, Foley, Everitt, Carr, Branston, Kiernan, Walden, Martin, Hall, Lines, Robson
- Sheffield Utd: Hodgkinson, Badger, Mallender, Munks, Shaw, Wagstaff, Docherty, Kettleboro', Jones, Birchenall, Reece

A temporary scaffolding stand is erected in front of the adjacent bowls club during the week to try to overcome the County Ground's spectator limitations. On the pitch, full-back Mallender intercepts Everitt's crossfield pass to thump home a 25-yard shot for a first ever league goal.

Match 13 — A LEEDS, 16/10 — 22 L 1-6 (1-3) — 33,748 — 2 6
- Best 14 [Lorimer 66, 75, Storrie 83] Bremner 20, Charl'n 43, Peacock 45, Leek
- Ref: R Tinkler
- Northampton: Harvey, Foley, Everitt, Kurila*, Carr, Kiernan, Best, Martin, Hunt, Leek, Robson
- Leeds: Sprake, Reaney, Bell, Bremner, Charlton, Hunter, Storrie, Lorimer, Peacock, Giles, O'Grady

The mistake here is taking the lead... Leeds are somewhat stung into action! Don Revie's side had just enjoyed a European baptism, beating Torino over two legs in the Fairs Cup. Despite the score, Hunt hits the woodwork twice, at 1-0 and 1-1, before Bremner and Giles take charge.

Match 14 — H WEST HAM, 23/10 — 21 W 2-1 (1-0) — 15,367 — 20 8
- Foley 29p, Leek 80 / Brown 49
- Ref: D Payne
- Northampton: Harvey, Foley, Cockcroft, Leek, Carr, Kiernan, Best, Leek, Hunt, Lines, Robson
- West Ham: Standen, Burnett, Charles, Peters, Brown, Moore, Brabrook, Bloomfield, Britt, Hurst, Sissons

West Ham had beaten Sheffield Wednesday 4-2 a week earlier, but the European Cup-Winners' Cup holders become the first Division One 'scalp', despite fielding six of the players which had defeated Munich 2-0 at Wembley. Hunt is fouled by Dennis Burnett for Foley's penalty.

Match 15 — A SUNDERLAND, 30/10 — 21 L 0-3 (0-2) — 32,216 — 13 8
- Martin 33, Gauden 37, Mulhall 75
- Ref: L Hamer
- Northampton: Harvey, Foley, Cockcroft, Leek, Carr, Kiernan, Walden, Leek, Hunt, Lines, Robson
- Sunderland: McLaughlin, Irwin, Parke, McNab, Baxter, Gauden, Herd, Martin, Moore, Mulhall

Neil Martin, a £45,000 signing from Hibernian scores on his home debut for Ian McColl's side who had dropped only one point at home in the league. Facing a gale in the first half, Bowen's men take a battering and are criticised for lack of effort, Walden putting in a transfer request.

Match 16 — H ASTON VILLA, 6/11 — 20 W 2-1 (2-0) — 18,836 — 12 10
- Hall 9, 10 / Park 63
- Ref: K Stokes
- Northampton: Coe, Foley, Cockcroft, Leek, Carr, Kiernan, Walden, Hall*, Hunt, Hunt, Robson
- Aston Villa: Withers, Wright, Aitken, Strong, Tindall, Deakin, Hamilton, Hateley, Park, Macleod, Scott

Hall returns the hero after a month out with a hamstring injury, while Coe has a first senior match in three seasons, thanks to Harvey's injury at Roker Park. Foley has four stitches in a cheek wound, sustained during a World Cup-tie in Spain. Leek has been sold to Bradford for £10,000.

Match 17 — A LIVERPOOL, 13/11 — 22 L 0-5 (0-3) — 41,904 — 1 10
- [Callaghan 63, Thompson 66/ St John 6, Stevenson 17p, Hunt 32,
- Ref: P Rhodes
- Northampton: Coe, Foley, Cockcroft, Leek, Carr, Branston, Kiernan, Walden, Hall, Hunt, Lines, Robson
- Liverpool: Lawrence, Lawler, Byrne, Strong, Yeats, Stevenson, Callaghan, Hunt, St John, Smith, Thompson

From the moment St John heads in Callaghan's sixth-minute corner there are no arguments. The champions elect are in a different league and the heroic Coe is given a rapturous send-off. Meanwhile, in the first FA Cup, non-league neighbours Bedford beat Third Division Exeter 2-1.

Match 18 — H TOTTENHAM, 20/11 — 22 L 0-2 (0-0) — 17,611 — 5 10
- Mackay 50, Saul 57
- Ref: R Aldous
- Northampton: Coe, Foley, Cockcroft, Kurila, Carr, Branston, Walden, Martin, Hall, Brown, Lines
- Tottenham: Jennings, Beal, Knowles, Mullery, Brown, Mackay, Possee, Clayton, Saul, Gilzean, Johnson

Outside-right Robson plays two days after signing from Ipswich, while Robson is being lined up for a move to Chelsea. Tommy Docherty drives up the M1 when their match with Sunderland is postponed. No Greaves, but Spurs have ex-Cobblers skipper Laurie Brown in defence.

Match 19 — A FULHAM, 27/11 — 22 W 4-1 (2-1) — 11,389 — 21 12
- Brown 16, 48, 76, Hunt 43 / Haynes 40
- Ref: N Burtenshaw
- Northampton: Coe, Foley, Cockcroft, Kurila, Carr, Branston, Kiernan, Hunt, Hall, Brown, Robson
- Fulham: Macedo*, Cohen, Nichols, Haynes, Keetch, Callaghan, Marsh, Brown, Dempsey, Key, O'Connell, Dyson

Robson is deliberately included for Lines, so watching Chelsea coach Jimmy Andrews can assess him. Brown earns the plaudits though, his hat-trick helped by Macedo's injury, Marsh replacing him as a makeshift goalkeeper. Robson completes his move for £30,000 two days later.

Match 20 — H BLACKPOOL, 4/12 — 20 W 2-1 (0-0) — 14,504 — 18 14
- Broadfoot 47, Lines 51 / Ball 55p
- Ref: H New
- Northampton: Coe, Foley, Cockcroft, Kurila, Carr, Branston, Broadfoot, Hunt, Hall, Brown, Lines
- Blackpool: Waiters, Armfield, Thompson, McPhee, James, Green, Moir, Ball, Charnley, Robson, Horne

The Cobblers ride their luck on the back of Broadfoot's only Cobblers goal and a Lines strike on a day when Fulham and Blackburn both lose to allow Bowen's men to leapfrog two places. The visitors are incensed a last-minute equaliser is not awarded, believing it has crossed the line.

Match 21 — A BLACKBURN, 11/12 — 21 L 1-6 (1-5) — 10,685 — 19 14
- Lines 44 [England 33, Harrison 52p] Ferguson 7, Jones 23, 25, 39,
- Ref: R Egan
- Northampton: Coe, Foley, Cockcroft, Kurila, Carr, Branston, Broadfoot, Hunt, Hall, Brown, Lines
- Blackburn: Else, Wilson, Newton, Clayton, Mulvaney, Sharples, Darling, Jones, England, Ferguson, Harrison

Blackburn's previous home games have brought wins over Newcastle (4-2) and Nottingham Forest (5-0) and here, George Marshall's men even have another Harrison goal ruled out as the half-time whistle goes. The Cobblers sign Graham Moore for £15,000 from Manchester Utd.

LEAGUE DIVISION 1 Manager: Dave Bowen SEASON 1965-66

No	Date			Att	Pos	Pt	F-A	H-T	Scorers, Times, and Referees	1	2	3	4	5	6	7	8	9	10	11	12 sub used
22	27/12	H	CHELSEA	23,325	21 9	L 14	2-3	0-0	Brown 59, Moore 79 / Tambling 67, 77, Graham 84 / Ref: D Corbet	Coe	Everitt	Cockcroft	Carr	Branston	Kiernan	Broadfoot	**Moore**	Hall	Brown	Lines	
										Bonetti	_Harris_	_McCreadie_	_Hollins_	_Hinton_	_Boyle_	_Bridges_	_Graham_	_Osgood_	_Venables_	_Tambling_	
23	28/12	A	CHELSEA	17,635	21 9	L 14	0-1	0-0	Bridges 83 / Ref: L Callaghan	Coe	Foley	Everitt	Carr	Branston	Kiernan	Broadfoot	**Moore**	Brown	Martin	Lines	
										Bonetti	_Harris_	_McCreadie_	_Hollins_	_Hinton_	_Boyle_	_Bridges_	_Graham_	_Osgood_	_Venables_	_Robson_	
24	1/1	A	SHEFFIELD UTD	16,143	20 9	D 15	2-2	1-1	Lines 13, Martin 66 / Jones 11, 51 / Ref: W Crossley	Coe	Cockcroft	Everitt	Carr	Branston	Kiernan	Broadfoot	**Moore**	Brown	Martin	Lines	
										Hodgkinson	_Badger_	_Mallender_	_Matthewson_	_Shaw_	_Wagstaff B_	_Reece_	_Kettlebora' Jones_	_Wagstaff T_	_Hartle_		
25	8/1	H	BLACKBURN	15,820	20 21	W 17	2-1	2-0	Kiernan 44, Brown 45 / Sharples 56 / Ref: A Weller	Coe	Foley	Everitt	Carr	Branston	Kiernan	Broadfoot	**Moore**	Brown	Martin	Lines	
										Else	_Wilson_	_Joyce_	_Newton_	_Mulvaney_	_Clayton_	_Darling_	_Jones *_	_England_	_Ferguson_	_Harrison_	_Sharples_
26	15/1	A	WEST HAM	20,745	20 17	D 18	1-1	1-1	Brown 15 / Hurst 37p / Ref: P Walters	Coe	Foley	Everitt	Carr	Branston	Kiernan	Broadfoot	**Moore**	Brown	Hall	Lines	
										Standen	_Burnett_	_Burkett_	_Bovington_	_Brown_	_Moore_	_Brabrook_	_Peters_	_Britt_	_Hurst_	_Dear_	
27	29/1	H	EVERTON	16,309	20 11	L 18	0-2	0-2	Temple 2, Scott 41 / Ref: K Styles	Coe	Cockcroft	Everitt	Carr	Branston	Kiernan	Moore	Hall	Broadfoot	Brown	Lines	
										West	_Wright_	_Wilson_	_Gabriel_	_Labone_	_Harris_	_Young_	_Harvey_	_Scott_	_Pickering_	_Temple_	
28	5/2	A	MANCHESTER U	35,273	20 3	L 18	2-6	1-4	Moore 23, Martin 56 [Connelly 10,] Law 5, 46, Charlton 28, 30, 85, / Ref: H Hackney	Coe	Cockcroft	Everitt	Kurila	Carr	Kiernan	Broadfoot	**Moore**	Hall	Martin	Lines	
										Gregg	_Dunne_	_Cantwell_	_Crerand_	_Foulkes_	_Stiles_	_Best_	_Law_	_Charlton_	_Herd_	_Connelly_	
29	12/2	A	STOKE	16,522	20 8	L 18	2-6	1-3	Moore 27, Brown 82 [Dobing 42] Ritchie 1, 65p, 70, 87, Vernon 31, / Ref: K Stokes	Coe	Foley	Everitt	Cockcroft	Carr	Kiernan	Broadfoot	**Moore**	Brown	Martin	Lines	
										Farmer	_Palmer_	_Allen_	_Viollet_	_Setters_	_Skeels_	_Bebbington_	_Dobing_	_Ritchie_	_Vernon_	_Jones_	
30	19/2	H	NEWCASTLE	14,541	20 18	W 20	3-1	2-0	Martin 15, 54, Moore 32 / Iley 90 / Ref: G Davis	Harvey	Foley	Everitt	Kurila	Branston	Kiernan	Broadfoot	**Moore**	Brown	Martin	Lines	
										Marshall	_Craig_	_Clark_	_Moncur_	_McGrath_	_Iley_	_Hilley_	_Suddick_	_Bennett *_	_Kettlebora' Robson_	_Noble_	
31	26/2	A	WEST BROM	18,923	20 7	D 21	1-1	1-1	Martin 8 / Clark 22 / Ref: L Faulkner	Harvey	Foley	Everitt	Kurila	Branston	Kiernan	Broadfoot	**Moore**	Brown	Martin	Lines	
										Potter	_Fairfax_	_Williams_	_Lovett_	_Jones_	_Fraser_	_Brown_	_Howshall *_	_Kaye_	_Crawford_	_Clark_	_Collard_

22 Was this the Cobblers' largest ever crowd? Officially no, but a gate is broken at the Wantage Road end and plenty see the match 'free'. Moore scores on his debut but a bad 84th-minute flare-up leaves Tambling out cold, Branston writhing on the ground and Chelsea grabbing a winner.

23 Tambling is missing from the return after the death of his father, so Robson appears against his old team-mates. Bonetti defies the Cobblers throughout, but is powerless when Brown hits the bar from a Lines corner. Bridges back-heads a Venables cross over Coe for the late winner.

24 Familiar surroundings in a three-sided football ground help the Cobblers feel at home. This is the only Division One point the club has ever secured north of the Midlands, and it is earned without skipper Foley. A throat infection ends his sequence of 88 consecutive league games.

25 Smith's men aren't the only 'Rovers' at the County Ground as there is a pre-match display by the RAF Police Dog Team. The down-at-heel visitors are sent packing (revenge sweet) after a lively contest, the feature of which is a battle between the 'big men' Branston and England.

26 The Cobblers' mid-winter break is a three day stop at Broadstairs prior to this visit. Somehow the match went ahead, despite the snow. Bowen uses the old 'baseball boot' ruse, so successfully employed against Sunderland two seasons earlier. Again, it helps balance on a hard surface.

27 Everton had beaten Sunderland 3-0 in the FA Cup a week earlier, and are destined for great things at Wembley in May. This is a poor game though, Temple nudging the visitors ahead when Branston misjudges a Gordon West free-kick, the ball ultimately bouncing over Coe's head.

28 United had been beaten only once in two years at Old Trafford and had beaten Benfica 1-0 in the European Cup quarter-final first leg on the Wednesday night, watched by Bowen and assistant Joe Payne. Moore scores against his old club while Martin side-foots in a Broadfoot cross.

29 Coe is pole-axed in the first minute, former Kettering striker John Ritchie scoring in the process. Cockcroft deputises for Foley, with Everitt moving across to right-back. Michael Beesley writes: 'It is hard to reconcile last season's well-disciplined rearguard with the same players.'

30 The Geordies had taken seven points from their previous four games but there was a breath of fresh air at the County Ground with Harvey, Foley and Branston all returning from injuries. Kurila was outstanding at the back, and Newcastle only made the scoresheet with the last kick.

31 Two pitch inspections are needed before this goes ahead amid deep mud and pools of water. 'Lake Hawthorns' looks like being a lucky venue, but Jimmy Hagan's side are free-scoring even without Astle, and when Harvey drops a Kaye shot, left winger Clark nets the rebound.

Match record (column headers): Harvey | Foley | Everitt | Kurila | Branston | Kiernan | Broadfoot | **Moore** | **Hudson** | **Martin** | Lines

---

32 · H · LEEDS · 5/3 — Att 21,548 · 19 W (3) 23 · **2-1**
Lines 11, Hudson 13 / *O'Grady 15* · Ref: T Dawes

Home: Harvey · Foley · Everitt · Kurila · Branston · Kiernan · Broadfoot · Moore · Hudson · Martin · Lines
Away: *Sprake · Reaney · Bell · Bremner · Charlton · Hunter · O'Grady · Lorimer · Storrie · Giles · Cooper*

Division One masterclass! Leeds had beaten Ujpest Dozsa 4-1 on the Wednesday to reach the semi-finals of the Fairs Cup but that gloss is dimmed by debut striker George Hudson from Coventry, who crosses for Lines' opener before bamboozling Jackie Charlton for the second.

---

33 · H · NOTT'M FOREST · 12/3 — Att 18,670 · 18 D (15) 24 · **3-3**
Martin 17, Moore 49, Kurila 89 / *Baker 6, 86, Storey-Moore 60* · Ref: H Richards

Home: Harvey · Foley · Everitt · Kurila · Branston · Kiernan · Walden · Moore · Hudson · Martin · Lines
Away: *Grummitt · Brindley · Newton · Hennessey · McKinlay · Whitefoot · Storey-Moore · Crowe · Baker · Barnwell · Hinton*

A poetic sense of justice as Kurila salvages a late point after two shots are charged down in a penalty box scramble. Forest had achieved something similar in the draw at the City Ground. England centre-forward Joe Baker makes his debut after a £65,000 move from Arsenal.

---

34 · A · SHEFFIELD WED · 19/3 — Att 16,263 · 20 L (16) 24 · **1-3**
Hudson 77 / *Ford 38, 86, Fantham 51* · Ref: E Norman

Home: Harvey · Foley · Everitt · Kurila · Branston · Kiernan · Broadfoot · Moore · Hudson · Martin · Lines*
Away: *Wicks · Smith · Megson · Eustace · Mobley · Young · Wilkinson · Fantham · Quinn · Ford · Dobson*

There are no arguments about The Owls' first league win at Hillsborough in 1966. The display is described as 'disinterested' and sends alarm bells ringing once more. Injuries to Lines and Foley prompts Mackin's debut, the versatile Corby youngster switching from attack to full-back.

---

35 · H · LEICESTER · 26/3 — Att 21,564 · 20 D (11) 25 · **2-2**
Hudson 3, Moore 40 / *Stringfellow 21, Sinclair 65* · Ref: R Paine

Home: Harvey · Foley* · Everitt · Kurila · Branston · Kiernan · Walden · Moore · Hudson · Martin · Mackin
Away: *Banks · Rodrigues · Norman · Roberts · Sjoberg · Cross · Sinclair · Matthews · Dougan · Gibson · Stringfellow*

Another experiment with Saturday night football which coincides with Anglo's Grand National victory at Aintree in the afternoon. It fails to bring the desired result, but Bowen's men hit the woodwork three times through Lines, Walden and Moore in a rip-roaring, frustrating finale.

---

36 · A · ASTON VILLA · 2/4 — Att 10,438 · 20 W (16) 27 · **2-1**
Mackin 48, Moore 62 / *Hamilton 13* · Ref: G McCabe

Home: Harvey · Mackin · Everitt · Kurila · Branston · Kiernan · Walden · Moore · Hudson · Martin · Lines
Away: *Gavan · Wright · Aitken · Tindall · Sleeuwenh'k · Deakin · Macleod* · Hamilton · Woosnam · Scott · Baker*

Camouflage tactics prevail as the Cobblers don an all white strip in the Villa Park blizzard. Mackin's 40-yard free-kick is misjudged by John Gavan, deputising for Colin Withers in goal while Moore, having scored the winner, nearly presents Tony Hateley with a 'back-pass' equaliser.

---

37 · H · LIVERPOOL · 9/4 — Att 20,029 · 20 D (1) 28 · **0-0**
Ref: P Walters

Home: Harvey · Mackin · Everitt · Kurila · Branston · Kiernan · Walden · Moore · Hudson · Martin · Lines
Away: *Lawrence · Lawler · Byrne · Smith · Yeats · Stevenson · Callaghan · Milne · St John · Strong · Thompson*

Roger Hunt is a late injury withdrawal. The England striker had damaged an ankle in the 4-3 win over Scotland at Hampden Park the previous Saturday and had aggravated it during the 1-0 midweek home win over Sheffield Wednesday. Ian St John needs early stitches in a face wound.

---

38 · H · STOKE · 12/4 — Att 20,680 · 20 W (10) 30 · **1-0**
Martin 49 · Ref: D Thomas

Home: Harvey · Mackin · Everitt · Kurila · Branston · Kiernan · Walden · Moore · Hudson · Martin · Lines
Away: *Farmer · Palmer · Skeels · Viollet · Setters · Kinnell · Bebbington · Dobing · Ritchie · Vernon · Burrows*

Wartime conflicts apart, this is Stoke's first visit for 44 years and the Cobblers' 50th Division One goal sends them away empty-handed. The victory is tempered by the fact Fulham have won 1-0 at title-chasing Leeds. Meanwhile, former youth international Carr asks for a transfer.

---

39 · A · TOTTENHAM · 16/4 — Att 29,749 · 20 D (8) 31 · **1-1**
Hudson 35 / *Greaves 78p* · Ref: K Walker

Home: Harvey* · Mackin · Everitt · Kurila · Branston · Kiernan · Walden · Hudson · Moore · Martin · Lines
Away: *Brown · Kinnear · Knowles · Mullery · Brown · Beal · Robertson · Greaves · Gilzean · Clayton · Possee*

Fulham's sudden remarkable run is proving a major irritant, even if the Cobblers' form is holding up. The Cottagers beat Sheffield Wednesday 4-2, which detracts from this excellent point, achieved after Harvey is forced off after an hour, leaving Mackin to take over between the sticks.

---

40 · H · FULHAM · 23/4 — Att 24,523 · 21 L (20) 31 · **2-4**
Martin 13, Kiernan 31 / *Robson 19, Earle 64, 87, 90* · Ref: J Taylor

Home: Coe · Mackin · Everitt · Kurila · Branston · Kiernan · Moore · Walden · Hudson · Martin · Lines
Away: *McClelland · Cohen · Nichols · Robson · Dempsey · Brown · Earle · Clarke · Haynes · Pearson · Leggat*

'Sorry Joe, I didn't see it, I can't give it.' The words of referee Jack Taylor to Kiernan as appeals for a 'behind the line' goal to bring a 3-1 lead are squashed. A glance across to the linesman proves equally hopeless. He has chosen that moment to fall over. Going down indeed....

---

41 · H · SUNDERLAND · 25/4 — Att 17,921 · 18 W (15) 33 · **2-1**
Everitt 69, Hudson 72 / *Martin 28* · Ref: N Burtenshaw

Home: Harvey · Mackin · Everitt · Kurila · Branston · Kiernan · Walden · Moore · Hudson · Martin · Lines
Away: *Montgomery · Irwin · Ashurst · Parke · Harvey · McNab · Hallowell · Herd · Martin · Baxter · Mulhall*

The Wearsiders need a point to be safe but despite this victory the Cobblers require an avalanche of other results to go their way. Two goals in three minutes raise the Hotel End rafters a fraction, Everitt's 22-yard rocket going in off angle of post and bar before Hudson fires the winner.

---

42 · A · BLACKPOOL · 30/4 — Att 15,295 · 21 L (13) 33 · **0-3**
Lea 52, Moir 70, Ball 88p · Ref: E Crawford

Home: Harvey · Mackin · Everitt · Kurila · Branston · Kiernan · Walden · Moore · Hudson · Martin · Lines
Away: *Waters · Armfield · Thompson · Fisher · James · McPhee · Moir · Ball · Charnley · Waddell · Lea*

There is to be no miracle salvation, no final shoots of recovery at Bloomfield Road. Fans bask in the seaside sunshine and for 45 minutes, anything appears possible. Then Ball sets up Lea for the opener, Ian Moir hits a second and Ball rounds off the scoring. The final curtain falls.

Home Average 18,634
Away Average 23,746

LEAGUE DIVISION 1 (CUP-TIES)   Manager: Dave Bowen   SEASON 1965-66

League Cup		Att	F-A	H-T	Scorers, Times, and Referees	1	2	3	4	5	6	7	8	9	10	11	12 sub used
2 A BLACKBURN	21 W	8,814 1:22	1-0	0-0	Everitt 58	Harvey	Foley	Cockcroft	Kurila	Carr	Kiernan	Everitt	Hall	Brown	Lines	Robson	
21/9					Ref: R Windle	Else	Newton	Clayton	England	Sharples	Douglas	McEvoy		Jones	Byrom	Harrison	
3 A FULHAM	22 L	7,834 1:19	0-5	0-3	Dyson 18, 76p, Dempsey 28, 37, 47	Harvey	Foley	Everitt	Carr	Branston	Kiernan	Walden	Etheridge	Brown	Leek	Robson	
13/10					Ref: W Clements	Macedo	Cohen	Nichols	Pearson	Keetch	Robson	Key	Marsh	Dempsey	Haynes	Dyson	

The Cobblers midfield are dominant, with Kiernan, Everitt and Lines the outstanding men. It is Kiernan who provides the goal delivery for Everitt, playing out on the wing. This is one of only two all Division One second-round ties, with Sunderland defeating Sheffield United 2-1.

Makeshift striker Dempsey flattens the Cobblers who are labelled 'a shambles' in sections of the national press. Eventual League Cup winners West Brom are 4-2 victors at Leeds, while West Ham, who they beat 5-3 in the last two-legged final, defeat Mansfield 4-0 at Upton Park.

FA Cup		Att	F-A	H-T	Scorers, Times, and Referees	1	2	3	4	5	6	7	8	9	10	11	12 sub used
3 H NOTT'M FOREST	20 L	17,873 1:12	1-2	1-1	Brown 32	Coe	Foley	Everitt	Carr	Branston	Kiernan	Broadfoot	Moore	Brown	Hall	Lines	
22/1					Crowe 29, Wignall 68	Cargill	Hindley	Newton	Hennessey	McKinlay	Whitefoot	Crowe	McArthur	Wignall	Barnwell	Hinton	
					Ref: K Howley												

The Cobblers are drawn at home in the FA Cup for the first time since 1962 and for the first time in the third round since the famous 3-1 win over Arsenal in 1958. Guest of honour is FIFA President Sir Stanley Rous, who sees Brown head in a Lines cross for the first-half equaliser.

Football Season — Final Tables

League Table

	Team	P	Home					Away					Pts
			W	D	L	F	A	W	D	L	F	A	
1	Liverpool	42	17	2	2	52	15	9	7	5	27	19	61
2	Leeds	42	14	4	3	49	15	9	5	7	30	23	55
3	Burnley	42	15	3	3	45	20	8	6	7	34	27	55
4	Manchester U	42	12	8	1	50	20	6	7	8	34	39	51
5	Chelsea	42	11	4	6	30	21	8	7	6	35	32	51
6	West Brom	42	11	6	4	58	34	8	6	7	40	37	50
7	Leicester	42	12	4	5	40	28	7	7	7	20	29	49
8	Tottenham	42	11	6	4	55	37	6	4	11	19	34	44
9	Sheffield Utd	42	11	6	4	37	25	5	5	11	23	42	43
10	Stoke	42	12	6	3	42	22	4	4	13	17	43	42
11	Everton	42	12	6	3	39	19	3	5	13	24	50	41
12	West Ham	42	12	5	4	46	33	4	2	15	19	36	39
13	Blackpool	42	8	9	5	36	29	5	2	14	26	44	37
14	Arsenal	42	8	8	5	36	31	4	5	12	24	43	37
15	Newcastle	42	10	5	6	26	20	4	4	13	30	46	37
16	Aston Villa	42	10	3	8	39	34	5	3	13	21	48	36
17	Sheffield Wed	42	11	6	4	35	18	3	2	16	25	48	36
18	Nott'm Forest	42	11	3	7	31	26	4	3	13	25	46	36
19	Sunderland	42	13	2	6	36	28	1	6	14	15	44	36
20	Fulham	42	9	4	8	34	37	5	3	13	33	48	35
21	NORTH'TON	42	8	6	7	31	32	2	7	12	24	60	33
22	Blackburn	42	6	1	14	30	36	2	3	16	27	52	20
		924	245	103	114	877	580	114	103	245	580	877	924

Appearances and Goals

Player	Appearances						Goals			
	Lge	Sub	LC	Sub	FAC	Sub	Lge	LC	FAC	Tot
Best, Billy	4						1			1
Branston, Terry	27	1	1		1		1			1
Broadfoot, Joe	17			1			1			1
Brown, Bobby	22		2	1			9		1	10
Carr, Graham	27		2	1						
Cockcroft, Vic	17	1	1	1			1			1
Coe, Norman	15									
Etheridge, Brian			1							
Everitt, Mike	31	1	2	1			1	1		2
Foley, Theo	31		2	2			2			2
Hall, Jim	14	1	1	1			3			3
Harvey, Bryan	27		2	2						
Hudson, George	11						6			6
Hunt, Bobby	13						3			3
Kiernan, Joe	42		2	2			2			2
Kurila, John	20		1	1			1			1
Leck, Derek	11									
Leek, Ken	3		1				1			1
Lines, Barry	40			1			5			5
Livesey, Charlie	3						1			1
Mackin, John	7	2					1			1
Martin, Don	25			1			7			7
Moore, Graham	21						7			7
Robson, Tommy	15	1	2				3			3
Walden, Harry	19	1								
25 players used	462	7	22		11		55	1	1	57

Odds & ends

Double wins: (1) Aston Villa.

Double losses: (3) Everton, Burnley, Chelsea.

Won from behind: (2) Aston Villa (a), Sunderland (h).

Lost from in front: (4) Burnley (h), Chelsea (h), Leeds (a), Fulham (h).

High spots: Mixing it in the big league.
Recording a home win over eventual league runners-up Leeds.
Chalking up a league double over Aston Villa.
Attracting record attendances for Manchester Utd, Chelsea and Fulham.
Drawing at Arsenal, Tottenham and West Ham, to name but three.

Low spots: Failing to win in Division One until the 14th attempt.
Shipping 92 league goals – four more than Blackburn, 13 points behind.
Six-goal hammerings by Leeds, Blackburn, Manchester Utd and Stoke.
Regular injury disruptions to the defence. Bryan Harvey, Terry
Branston, Theo Foley and Mike Everitt were previously the linchpins.

Ever-presents: (1) Joe Kiernan.

Hat-tricks: (1) Bobby Brown (v Fulham).

Opposing hat-tricks: (7) Willie Irvine (Burnley), Jeff Astle (West Brom),
George Jones (Blackburn), Bobby Charlton (Manchester Utd),
John Ritchie (Stoke), Steve Earle (Fulham), John Dempsey (Fulham) LC.

Leading scorer: (10) Bobby Brown.

Dennis Adams	Theo Foley	Bill Craven	Joe Kiernan
John R Allen	Bryan Harvey	John Crouch	
Abraham Anstruther	Joe Kiernan	Geoff Crowson	Billy Best
Les Arnett	Bryan Harvey	J T Cutler	Whole Team
Andrew Ashley		Ian Davies	Mike Everitt
Martin Atwill	Joe Kiernan	A J Day	Joe Kiernan
Peter Austen	Joe Kiernan	Dave Drage	Joe Kiernan
Roger Averill	Joe Kiernan	Simon Draper	Joe Kiernan
Stewart Conrad Bailey		Colin Eldred	Bobby Brown
	Theo Foley	Steve Ellis	Joe Kiernan
James Baker		Brian Etheridge	Whole Team
Mark & Melanie Bamford		Peter Evans	
	Bryan Harvey	Stewart Farmer	Joe Kiernan
Martin Banks	Don Martin	Andrew Finch	Bryan Harvey
Chris Barritt	Dave Bowen	Michael Charles Fitzhugh	
Bill Beesley	Joe Kiernan		Don Martin
Donald Beesley	Theo Foley	Alan Frampton	Theo Foley
Grace Lillian Florence Beesley		James Frampton	Theo Foley
Mary Beesley	Theo Foley	Dayn G Freeman	Whole Team
Arnie Bell	Joe Kiernan	Jane & Mark French	
Chris Bell	Joe Kiernan	Peter Glithero	Don Martin
Keith J Bell	Joe Kiernan	N E Goss	Whole Team
Paul Bell	Dave Bowen	Justine Grande	Dave Bowen
Bob & Liz Bilson	Joe Kiernan	Mark Gray	Joe Kiernan
Trevor Bilson	Mike Everitt	Michael Green	Theo Foley
Norman Boyling	Theo Foley	Richard Green	Theo Foley
Philip Breed		D J Hakes	Joe Kiernan
David Britten		Steve Hamlyn	Derek Leck
Andrew Bubeer		Les Hawkins	Theo Foley
Geoff Butcher	Joe Kiernan	John Hay	
Mark Causebrook	Joe Kiernan	Nick Haycox	Bryan Harvey
John Chapman	Theo Foley	Stephen R Haynes	Joe Kiernan
Andrew Charter	Joe Kiernan	A J Hiskey	Joe Kiernan
Lee & Martin Childs	Graham Carr	Steve Hollowell	Jim Hall
Steve Church	Joe Kiernan	Brian Humphrey	Joe Kiernan
Barrie Clarke	Theo Foley	Andy Ingman	
John (Nobby) NTFC Clarke		Martyn Ingram	Joe Kiernan
	Theo Foley	Tom Ingram	Joe Kiernan
J H Coles	Theo Foley	Gorden F Inwood	Joe Kiernan
Robert Cook	Terry Branston	Peter Isham	Graham Moore
Clem Cooper	Theo Foley	Neil Ives	Joe Kiernan
Ian Cooper	Whole Team	Robert Johnson	Joe Kiernan
John M Cosford	Barry Lines	Alan Kerr	Theo Foley

A C Kingston	Joe Kiernan	Maurice Ribbans	Joe Kiernan
Edwin & Kieran Lane		William Rich	Don Martin
Jean Leck		Nick Richards	Joe Kiernan
Dave Letts	Theo Foley	Steve Riches	Theo Foley
Darren Lewis	Joe Kiernan	Keith Rimmington	Bryan Harvey
Henry W Liddington	Graham Moore	Richard Rimmington	Bryan Harvey
Barry Lines	Graham Moore	Richard K Rimmington	
Ron Linsdell			Joe Kiernan
Andrew Little	Joe Kiernan	Andy Roberts	Theo Foley
Andy Love	Joe Kiernan	Roy Robinson	Theo Foley
Tony J Lyon	Theo Foley	Amy Rodhouse	Joe Kiernan
John Masters	Billy Best	Ben Rodhouse	Joe Kiernan
Peter D Matcham	Joe Kiernan	Jason Rodhouse	Joe Kiernan
Alan May	Joe Kiernan	Steve Rodhouse	Joe Kiernan
John Mayes	Dave Bowen	Terry Rodhouse	Joe Kiernan
Dale McCann	Joe Kiernan	Dorothy Ronson	Joe Kiernan
Stan Monk	Theo Foley	Martin Rose	Theo Foley
Andrew Morris	Theo Foley	John E Rowe	Joe Kiernan
John Morris	Theo Foley	Alan Rowles	Joe Kiernan
Rob Mortimer	Joe Kiernan	John Ruff	Joe Kiernan
Geoffrey Moss	Joe Kiernan	Colin Russell	Joe Kiernan
Bob Murray	Joe Kiernan	R J Russell	Joe Kiernan
D J Nash		Ralph Sheridan	Joe Kiernan
Richard Newman	Joe Kiernan	Derek Shurville	Joe Kiernan
Tom O`Reilly		Martin Simmonds	
Dr Derek Oakensen		Steve Simmonds	Joe Kiernan
John A Oakensen		Ed Slinn	Joe Kiernan
Simon Oliver	Joe Kiernan	Carl Smith	
Keith Onley		Linda Smith	
Colin Osborne	Joe Kiernan	John Spencer	Barry Lines
Stuart Parker		Robert Spick	Bryan Harvey
Iain Paterson		Roger Springett	
Philip Paterson	Barry Lines	Arthur Stamp	Joe Kiernan
Liam Pattinson	Graham Carr	Robert Stamp	Terry Branston
Bob Payne		Bhyll Stephenson	
F Payne	Bryan Harvey	Anthony Stimpson	Joe Kiernan
David Phillips	Joe Kiernan	Clive Stock	Joe Kiernan
Anthony C Platt	Joe Kiernan	Russell Sturgen	Joe Kiernan
Glenn James Powell	Theo Foley	Barry & Betty Summers	
Tony Price	Barry Lines		Joe Kiernan
William Rangeley	Joe Kiernan	Nod Sumpter	Whole Team
Chris Reed		Nick Swannell	Theo Foley
Bill Ribbans	Joe Kiernan	W J Swingler	

Michael Tack	Joe Kiernan	*Harvey Wells*	Theo Foley
Michael Taylor	Theo Foley	*Katrina J Wells*	Joe Kiernan
Terry Tebbutt	Theo Foley	*Keith & Ann West*	Joe Kiernan
Philip Thompson	Joe Kiernan	*Mick White*	Theo Foley
Dave Thorn	Theo Foley	*D Wills*	Joe Kiernan
Gill Turland	Theo Foley	*Tony Wilson*	Joe Kiernan
John Upson		*Don Wright*	Joe Kiernan
Chris Venes			
David Walden	Joe Kiernan		
Jackie Warner	Joe Kiernan	14 PLAYERS RECEIVED VOTES	
Alan Watson	Joe Kiernan	1st	Joe Kiernan
John Watson	Joe Kiernan	2nd	Theo Foley
Brian Webster	Bryan Harvey	3rd	Bryan Harvey

The first goal of Northampton's First Division career arrives after twenty minutes of the opening game at Goodison Park. Unfortunately, the scorer is Everton's Alex Young